The Bloody Sacrifice

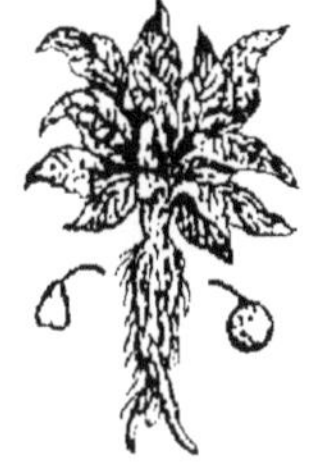

For Marie, Ian and Sara

True Magick does not exist without True Love.

And with thanks to

Eric K Lerner, Mogg Morgan and VisualAIDS

The Bloody Sacrifice

A Personal Experience of Contemporary Blood Rites

by
Charlotte Rodgers

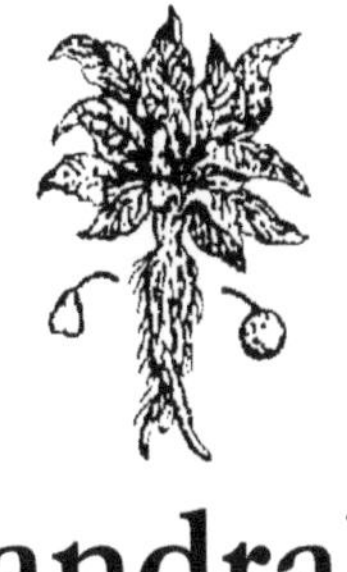

Mandrake

Published by
Mandrake of Oxford
PO Box 250
OXFORD
OX1 1AP (UK)
ISBN 978-1-906958-30-5

Contents

Introduction

I am a non denominational magickal practitioner and an animist and *The Bloody Sacrifice* is the story of my spiritual and creative work with blood, over a period of many years.

My spirituality has always been heavily focused on art and personal experience and my magickal practice is a combination of this and a long term preoccupation with blood based ritual. Whilst I do not fall under any umbrella term or conform to any practitioner type, I have found enough identification amongst certain traditions and enough success within my practice to realise the validity of my approach.

Initially I was aiming to write of only my own magickal and creative experiences using blood in a conscious spiritual context, however as I started to write I found that my vision necessarily expanded to include the voices of others.

I decided early on to use interviews as part of my research, a method which I've used before and found to be more fluid and responsive than simply relating personally experienced and studied information.

Some of the interviews I made were so intrinsic to the development of my blood work that I felt that it was essential that they be recorded in their entirety, whilst others I learned from but decided not to reproduce in this book.

One of the interviews I have included is with Louis Martinie, a priest in the New Orleans Voodoo Spiritual Temple who has integrated his

Tibetan Buddhist beliefs into his Voodoo practice. Martinie found non-sentient alternatives to blood sacrifice and in doing so shows how personal spiritual evolution can effect change within a syncretic religion.

To an extent I can empathise with Martinie's views, however my own experience of using blood in rituals has led me to believe that God-forms and spirits have very specific ways of working and strong preferences that, if not met, can cause 'difficult' behaviour.

I believe it will be fascinating to observe the changes as they occur within The New Orleans Voodoo Spiritual Temple, and note any long term effects that the loa's new diet produces.

As a blood related illness affected various parts of my life, I was given a chance to explore blood ritual in a very different way and this led to my contact with various HIV positive artists and the Santero Eric K Lerner. I feel that documenting this part of the journey was vital to help create an understanding of what blood rites are and where they can take you and also give an insight into the concept of 'dis-eased' blood such as AIDS, HIV and HCV, and its effect on spirituality.

The section on body art, mortifications and modifications represents a vital aspect of contemporary culture which has also been a part of my own processes of transformation.

It may be remiss of me not to mention the work of artists such as Orlan, Hermann Nitsch, or Marina Abramnovic (to name but a few), all of whom use blood in their art work. I appreciate their work on a creative and philosophical level but it did not move me to the extent that I felt it necessary to include in this book.

Another seemingly glaring omission could be seen to be that of the work of Genesis Breyer P-Orridge; however I feel I have given appropriate mention of his huge contribution in this area in the citations.

The contents of this book may be considered to be more about occulture than the occult but just as no human being lives within a vacuum, no true magician ignores emphasis on creative magickal expression within their practice.

I have made an attempt to present the huge amount of related subject matter by dividing the book into three sections and an addendum ('The Spaces In-between')

Mortification, Art, and Sacrifice are again divided into sections with an introduction followed by my personal experiences.

I also include in these chapters, interviews and some wonderful, evocative and very affecting images.

The final chapter, 'The Spaces In-between' contains the interview with Yoruba priest Eric K Lerner, who has been a huge source of inspiration and information for me whilst I compiled this tome.

I then close the book with Mogg Morgan's 'Blood on the Threshold: Seth The Demonic Initiator'.

In this essay Mogg tries to dispense with cultural detail and seek the universal pattern in blood rites; something that speaks directly to the living phenomenon that is the magician. In doing this he ventures into the realm of the god Set and explores the theme of ambiguity.

The way in which I have divided the subject matter in the name of necessary organisation of the mass of information, is very much subject to my own personal interpretations of classification. Putting my work with menstrual blood under the category of *Sacrifice* is one such example.

Whilst I am a voracious reader, this book reflects rather than records my related academic study. I initially used footnotes in the chapters but decided that this added a scholarly aspect which was a distraction from the creative and magickal elements which I wanted emphasised, so I removed them and instead included a comprehensive bibliography of my references.

My long absorption with this subject has had profound emotional and physical effects on me, some of which have been difficult in the process but wonderful in eventual effect.

This effect was due not only to my ritual magickal practise but also to the art, research, and conversations that lay behind the creation of *The Bloody Sacrifice*.

Now that this book is finished so also is completed a phase in my creative and magickal life.

I realise that my immersion in this particular subject was in my early years, in part about challenging taboos, although my pull to work in this manner was actually inherent.

Body modification and tattoo art is no longer considered unacceptable as it was in my teens, however I found when I talked to younger people involved in such practices, little has really changed at a core level.

Whatever the initial reasons for performing blood rituals, there is no doubt that it is an atavistic act. This act, with all its history, baggage and dangers holds a power that has the capacity to create change. Whether this power is held within blood itself, and how much impact is created by our perception of the substance, is part of your own decision process; something I hope this book can illuminate.

Art

'Spirituality and Art are one and the same. Works of art are prayers at the altar of life.' Raquelin Mendieta

The historical use of blood in art, even in sacred art is rarer than one would think. Blood is a contradiction, something which is considered to carry life and death, the sacred and the profane. It is ingrained within a general human consciousness with an accompanying mythology and a wariness which prevents its casual use.

Bones and remnants of death are more common as an artistic and creative medium, but still tended to be regulated to the realms of representation of the sacred.

The 20th century changed this attitude somewhat, as it attempted to utilise the taboo that is engendered within blood and use that as social and political commentary as well as art work.

Pioneered by the surrealists, by the 60s and 70s art which utilised blood, especially within performance, whilst relatively underground and invariably controversial was not that unusual.

Dismemberment of animals; facial mutilation with razor blades; drawing blood with hypodermic syringes to be mixed with urine, hair and nail clippings and then drunk; and kitchen table castrations were only some of the performances that were shown as art works during this time.

The advent of AIDS created new attitudes and fears associated with blood, or perhaps simply awakened old, atavistic terrors.

If you work with blood does it change you?

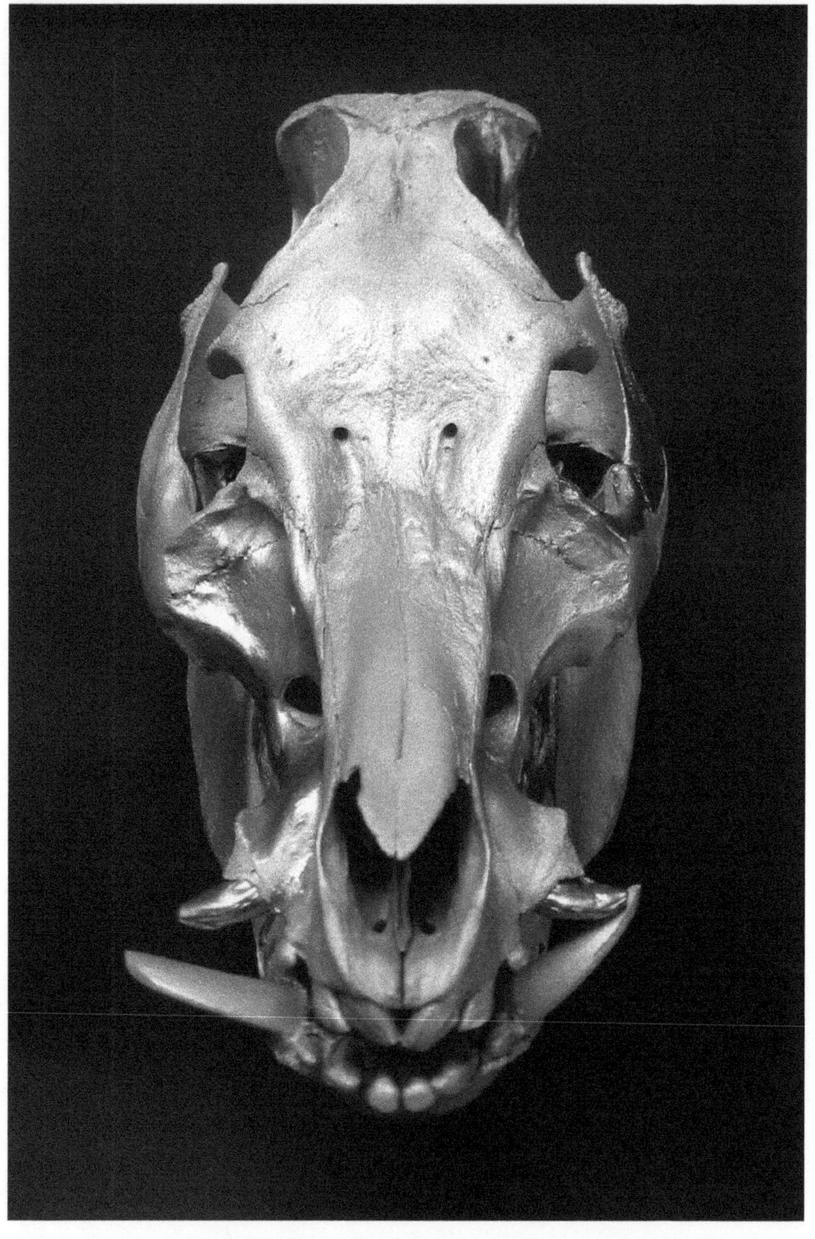

'Prosperity Pig' & 'Prosperity Pig Innards'
Mixed Media with Boar's Skull by Charlotte Rodgers.

Personal

As a child I had a fascination with the unseen and the forbidden. I was enamoured with bones, the residue of death and other sundries that could be considered dirty, unsavoury and nasty.

At the age of seven I dragged home a ram's skull which I had found in a deserted mine and later that year discovered the magazine *Man Myth and Magic.*

The parental reaction to both incidents was explosively negative to say the least and gradually I realised that my perspectives and the places in which I was comfortable were not considered acceptable, normal or healthy.

Authoritative figures railed at me for considered wrong behaviours and attitudes. The more alienated and lonely I felt for being this way, the more I adopted standard reactionary behaviour such as eating disorders and drug addiction. As behaviour modifications, treatment centres and therapy released me from the aforementioned antisocial and destructive habits I found myself becoming increasingly lonely and empty. I was not suffering from depression but from a feeling of loss.

I realised an irony in that my various multi therapies resulted in the real me emerging and this 'me' was the same persona that had created the initial problems as a reaction to lack of acceptance within mainstream society.

This aspect of self loved bones, dead things, playing games of worship in the fields and believed in myth and magic.

As long as this part of me was unacknowledged it was natural I would feel loss so I decided it was time to allow this child to resurface, so that I could finally be whole.

I also decided to return to the magick and the art that was at my centre and accept that as my truth. In keeping with this decision, I started to create fetish objects for the first time in 20 years.

In my late teens I had worked with taxidermy and mummification techniques and through trial and messy pungent error, I learned the best way to preserve the road kill that I found.

I taught myself camouflage and dazzling painting techniques to bring out the essence of skulls and bones and rearrange that essence into a working magickal formula. I adhered very much to the words of Hugh B. Cott, who said of art and camouflage (respectively) that "*the one makes something unreal recognizable [while] the other makes something real unrecognizable*," except I enlarged upon art and camouflage to include magick.

When I was 18 I experimented with an amalgamation of dead animal's parts to create an army. Bear in mind these were the days when *2000AD*, *Psychic TV*, *Modern Primitives* and industrial music ruled so there was admittedly a *Mad Max* quality in what I made.

I used the heavy viciousness of possum bones as the foot soldiers, long legged wading birds as vehicles, and finer featured rats as lower officers. I painted them in personalised interpretations of camouflage colours and added my hair to some of them. They were named and placed in the ante room to my bedroom after being allotted the task of protecting me.

These creatures did watch over me during those unhappy years and when I left that particular home and country; living animals destroyed the bizarre fetish army which they had previously studiously avoided.

When I see a bone I see a gateway to the essence of the creature that it once belonged to. In my opinion individuality departs on or around the moment of death, and the remnant of the once living form becomes a reminder which can act as a link to a deeper and more permanent essence of species.

Sometimes there may have been a trauma in death that causes the individual soul or spirit to linger longer than usual. This is something which can easily be worked with and released.

When I look at bones and especially skulls I see something that is a holder of energy. This could be is why I am so good at finding them as I look for the energy rather than the receptacle that contains it.

As an aside I would say that the most disturbing piece that I have had in my collection is not a human, but a baboon's skull. The similarity between human and ape is strong and the baboon embodying such base brutality and violence is an unnerving reminder of human capacity.

Once I decided to start working with the art of fetish again, I retrained myself in camouflage techniques by working with lightening struck wood with strange and twisted shapes. I used metallic paint to highlight the wood's elemental essence so that my medium's true nature would become visible to eyes other than my own.

Then I started making spirit houses. My aim was to create from a skull an object which worked with energy. I aimed to capture some of this energy and transform it before release, whilst retaining that which was unwanted or could be considered detrimental.

For instance I'd work on a spirit house that would stand at an entrance to a home. The main body of the spirit house would be a ram's skull (martial solidity for protection) with a mummified magpie's head fused to it (magpies are a traditional theft repellents, sympathetic magick to put it plainly).

Then I would seal the whole object together in reflective silver paint (intuitive lunar energy), and add a few beads and pieces of glitter to keep any playful spirits entertained.

I worked on a series of these to get my knack back, and then decided to be more experimental and integrate this work into my magickal practice. Around this time I was put on a course of medication called Pegasus that had a profound negative physical and psychological effect on me.

I was given a horse's skull and decided that it was appropriate to make a spirit house to capture and change the side effects of the chemotherapy into something more positive. Thus I created the 'N'mare: The Descent' a decidedly chthonic spirit house that aimed to hold pain and transform it into a more positive shamanic, journeying experience.

Originally I had been very loath to work with this skull as it was from an abattoir and I only work with road kill or natural death rather than something that was deliberately killed.

The hole in the mare's skull from the rivet murder method was particularly disturbing and after talking to friends who knew the way that abattoirs operated, it became even more so.

However I realised if I worked my own trauma through simultaneously with the horse's I should heal and transform us both

The skull was painted in silvers and blacks, with green-black bugle beads creating a decidedly fly blown effect. The horse's tail was made into a hair piece that gave the beast the martial quality that was necessary to fight its way to the light after its dark journeying.

Once the course of treatment was finished I discovered that it would be another six months before the toxins were out of my system so it seemed apt to create another piece to complement the mare. I crafted a 'Recovery Ship' to mark the completion of the transformation which the mare had started.

I began with the battered model of the ship *The Marie Rose*, found in the garage of a friend's newly bought house. The ship had obviously once been the focus of attention and love before damp, dust and neglect did their work.

I restored the boat then I changed it.

I crusted it in solar colours, gold beads and clear crystal.

The prow was lifted with a huge whale's vertebra and a biscuit porcelain Victorian doll's head was placed on the mast's top to gaze forward.

At either side of the boat I used ivory knights from an old chess set to tie in with the mare's head. On the prow I placed a large, old, and crazed wooden horse's head. Originally an Indian toy, its bright colours and lopsided lunatic grin made it the essence of the fool and the antithesis of the N'mare

It was interesting that the process of finishing the boat tied in exactly with the clearing of the medication from my system.

I would be on the verge of finishing completely when I would run out of a particular colour bead or be unable to locate another key ingredient. In one terrible instance I even stood on the sculpture (my workshop is in a very small area in my kitchen) and needed to start all over again.

I had channelled through automatic writing many years before but I found that the act of holding a pen or pencil and using words as a medium was contradictory to the aim of bypassing of the intellect to access other realms, so I decided to channel into clay.

At this point, despite doing deconditioning work on myself, I felt that I had residual religious indoctrination holding me back.

I determined to flow out this conditioning by turning off my head, and introducing stimulus to cause my subconscious to react. I moulded clay to allow what was reacting within me to move into what was being created.

My stimulus came from the music from *Current 93, Christ and the Pale Queens* and a marathon session studying the Luciferian and Lilith Mythos.

The result was a series of beautiful and very anguished female figures that I called the 'Lilith Workings' and considered to be Lilith in various stages of her fall.

They were painted in the appropriate camouflage colours and then individually embellished with animal parts.

One had badger's teeth and crow's feathers, another was resplendent with snake skin and fox teeth and another had bird's claws for arms.

I used these objects as meditative aids. One was baptised with blood. I believed that I would exorcise unwanted religious beliefs that lingered in me and once removed I could work with the energy that lingered in the resultant 'gap' to create something more positive.

The giving/baptising in blood was symbolic of the giving of life to this new phase of my development.

Unfortunately things did not work out as planned.

I couldn't say that I created a servitor, a golem or a magickal child because what I made even though it came from me was no longer in my control. Feeding the art-work with blood rather than linking us, gave it life and made me its food supply and thus lower on the power pyramid.

It was an interesting time.

I found myself pulled to feed this creature that lived on my altar. I quickly realised that I was not turning into an inveterate self harmer, but that the creature which I had created was growing in strength and as 'she' grew so did her appetite and her corresponding vociferous demands for food. All of this was accompanied by a chaotic series of incidents which occurred in my house at the time.

I became afflicted with a plague of flooding in my flat, the flat upstairs which leaked down into mine, and at one stage the water pipes in the road outside.

I went through three new washing machines in a year, twice had to replace my bathroom and kitchen floors, and had to repaint and plaster my bedroom and living room ceiling.

I also would feel drops of water fall onto me, with no particular cause or source.

Perhaps it was coincidence but these floods did not seem to have a related mundane cause and they occurred within a short time span.

I talked to other magickal practitioners from various persuasions about my problem and interestingly enough, the greatest identification came from two spheres of what could be considered to be very elemental magick, Voudon and Enochian.

I tried to destroy these creatures by trapping them in a box with a mirrored inside lid, then with burning, dismemberment, and burial.

However their influence lingered and a year or so later I was wandering in a remote area near Avebury when my companion pointed out something that a cow had dug out of the soft earth. A now faded coloured piece of clay from one of my Lilith's.

I realised that what I had made could not be destroyed but would remain for me to accept and work with. Each year the anniversary of the Lilith Workings is marked by a random event (generally a flood).

After this rather traumatic series of workings, I decided to simplify things and I started working with dolls.

I suspect the psychology of what I was doing was similar to the Lilith workings although not as conscious.

I also decided not to feed these creatures with blood.

As an aside I have used blood (both menstrual and venous) in my magickal workings and although it was problematic it produced nowhere near the degree of trouble that the Lilith workings did.

Initially I found working with the plastic or rubber difficult, as I was used to natural and animate materials which are easier to connect with.

I quickly realised that the doll was animated by centuries of humanity's focus on the idealised qualities of the infant expressed within them.

I would make an ink with dragon's blood to represent the doll's life blood and then work with the particular combination of energies that I wanted each of them to embody.

Then a coloured base would be painted over the ink, thus sealing in the circulatory system which I had installed.

This colour would represent the base intention of the doll, its elemental starting point, so each doll would have an initial colour of silver, gold or black.

At this point I got a feeling for what each doll wanted to become and would start to layer the dolls in glass based glitter, bones and fossils.

I called these creatures elemental conductors in that they would embody particular combinations of energy.

An example was a doll called a 'An Oracular Head' which was coloured in reds and silvers (cold fire) and encrusted in fox and rattlesnake bones; curled around the neck of this doll was a mummified rattlesnake head.

The purpose of this particular doll was to heighten creative and intuitive insight and add a directed quality to it.

An interesting element of working with such magickal art forms is the reaction to them.

Observing those who gravitate towards a piece and discovering that people find the dolls much more disturbing than the creations made from animal by-products, has been fascinating.

I suspect that the sanctity of infancy and childhood are much more iconoclast than those of death.

After years of working with smaller animals I was asked to skin and prepare several larger creatures for a friend who taught biology. Both of these animals weighed 60 lbs or so (I will not get specific about the species of these animals for various reasons although they were both road kill and perfectly legal) and I found that the preparation was very physical and required a near trance state of concentration.

There was a descent into a primal and atavistic consciousness whilst the skinning and gutting was being done (as these creatures were both very large there was a lot of physical activity involved in working with them), and a recognition at an innermost level of what was being worked with.

I experinced a connection with the essence of the animal and after the adrenaline rush of the physical labour had passed I would experience exhaustion far greater than could be considered normal.

I was journeying with, and to, the animal (in a way similar to when I worked with the bones but at a much more base and physical level) and learned quickly to be aware of those animals that came into my life and at what time so I could see the patterns of necessary identification.

An intriguing thing about this sort of work is the reaction of living animals. I live with three cats (two of whom are part feral) and a large dog and they all become skittish and nervous when I am engaged in my fetish work.

In theory one would think that the blood would excite them, but it doesn't. I believe they pick up on the ritual qualities of my activities and in some ways this negates any blood lust that it would normally arouse in them.

Interview with Keith Theriot

The New York based organisation *Visual AIDS* kindly put a posting in their newsletter asking for AIDS and HIV infected artists who used blood in their art-work to contact with me if they were willing to be interviewed on the subject.

I talked to many artists who used their blood in a variety of mediums but related particularly well to Keith Theriot and Steed Taylor whose interviews I have recorded in this section.

Keith Theriot (http://www.keiththeriot.com/) is a Louisiana born artist who was diagnosed HIV+ in 1989; he has lived with full-blown AIDS since 1994.

Were you an artist before your diagnosis as being HIV positive?
Yes, I have been painting since I was 4 years old, 45 years ago.

How did this diagnosis change your relationship with your art work and with the mediums you used in this work?
I went through a period, shortly after my diagnosis that I couldn't paint. Painting for me is opening up my soul and my diagnosis, along with so many friends who were sick and dying at the time (1989) made it impossible for me to open up. I did continue to "create" with collage, photo and lots of stream of consciousness poetry. After

a few years, I picked up the brush again and began working on paintings related to my friend's death. About this time, 1992, I was working in the studio and cut my finger on a staple from a stretched canvas. The blood fascinated me and I made a few strokes on paper with it, and incorporated a drawing of a dying man. I put it away and discovered it a few years later. I had assumed the blood would turn to dust, but it stayed pretty solid and had turned a brownish colour, sort of like a conti crayon. I began a few clinical trials as there were not many treatment options then and again, I was confronted with my blood from the constant lab draws. The irony of my AIDS tainted blood killing me, but keeping me alive kept playing over and over. I had a cancer diagnosis of Kaposi Sarcoma and my doctor advised me to get my affairs in order as I only had about 18 months left. With that in mind I decided to paint a series of self portraits in my own "bio hazardous" blood, to sort-of leave a part of me behind for posterity. Since then I've done three or four different sets, with the mood of the work changing according to what's happening currently.

From what I have seen of your body of work your medium varies; does using blood in your art 'feel' different for you?
Yes, very different. In all mediums I try to approach my work with a stream of consciousness or with no preconceived ideas; that way it stays current to what I am trying to process mentally. Painting in blood is very much like watercolour in the sense that, unlike acrylics, it's a one shot deal.

How has the public reacted to the work created with your own blood?

It varies. Some people are totally horrified and disgusted and are not afraid to say it. Some jump back when they realize what it is; afraid, I guess, that it will jump off the paper and attack them. I guess that's the point of this, to force people to think about it. Not in a judgmental way of saying "do this" or "don't do this", but merely "think about it". The other half of the viewers is very moved by it and transfers their own experiences: that is when the work becomes very powerful, people begin to relate and it becomes about them. I love that part.

Still others remain silent and need time to process it. Rarely do I sell these during the first night of an exhibition. People go home, process it, think about it, and then return with the decision that they have to have it. I have sold hundreds of them, but rarely on the first night.

Has creating such courageous and personal work as this series changed you?

I don't think of them as courageous, but thank you. I was driven by the self-expression and I had to do it or go insane. I think most creative people will understand that. We don't think of it as the end result as much as, let me try this and see what happens. As for changing me personally, I think it has made me see that I can influence people to think differently about confronting death and it that sense appreciate life.

To some degree all creative work is a reflection of the inner self of the artist; however your art strikes me as a more than usually honest expression of who you are ... Am I mistaken in that?

All art is a representation of the artist, especially with the idea of stream of consciousness. I have found that there are many universal truths/imagery/statements that people will relate to - if the artist is honest and lets the public see that part of themselves there becomes a common ground. I allow myself to be exposed in the work, who I am as a person, and that allows the viewer to transfer that freedom internally. They began to allow those questions and answers of immortality internally.

It is interesting looking at the names of the works in this series such as 'Aphrodite (A.M and P.M)', 'Pegasus' and 'Ascension, which all suggest a rising upwards. Is the subject matter related to its blood medium, or is that an aside (if possible?)

From the stream of consciousness approach, I don't consciously think about what it's going to be. However, the universal truths of looking forward or upward or whatever is going on in my life are ultimately reflected. And not necessarily due to the medium, more about what is currently happening.

Surely blood changes in colour over time: do you work this into your pieces?

It doesn't change that much once it dries. Maybe a little darker, and although some may find this a bit disgusting, it depends on how long I've had it. If it is fresh, say within a few weeks, it is bright red and remains that way. If I've had it for several months, it is darker. Both versions have great value and work for what I'm trying to do. I do not continuously think about it though.

Are you affiliated with a specific religion or spiritual practice?

I was born and raised Catholic, but ceased that sadomasochist practice when I left home to enter college at 17. I would have to admit that the "body and blood of Christ" ritual during each Catholic mass left a strong impression and my fascination with blood may be a result of having to endure that every Sunday for the first 16 years of my life. Since then I've done some spiritual/religious exploring, particularly after my AIDS diagnosis. This spiritual search led me to belief that everyone, every religion has it right and every religion has it wrong. The ultimate truth is that there is no truth and only what you believe. If you believe in heaven or hell, then when you die that is what you experience - because it's all in your mind. I believe that to achieve balance in *my* life I must nurture the three elements of mind, body and spirit - which is where the "Graces" idea originates mostly in my "non-Blood" artwork.

How does 'Bloodworks' fit within your spirituality?

Bloodwork fits into my practice of non-religious but spiritual belief in the sense that I connect with myself on spiritual/mind/body level to allow the work and imagery to flow naturally, without learned filters and rely on my internal spiritual controls.

Are you saying you are using an automatic or channelled method of creating your art work? Do you do this with all your work, or only the blood work?

Yes, in 98% of my work, I use a "stream of consciousness" approach. For me that is the most productive way to get to the core of who I am and share what I am feeling at the time.

I start with a very expressionistic application of paint, blood, whatever and let the figures or images emerge. Every painting becomes an internal self portrait. Not that the aim is to create only self portraits, but I have found that if I honestly produce work from the inside, it is more likely to relate on a universal level to the viewer's own experiences. We all confront similar issues - in our own way, on our own level, in our own time

Has your HIV status and blood work changed your approach to your spirituality?

My AIDS diagnosis forced me to confront my idea of what happens after death. For about a year I researched, attended rituals and sought out different belief systems. That is where I came to the conclusion for myself that it's all in one's mind. The idea of using blood did not happen until after my HIV diagnosis and on a much stronger, relevant level after my AIDS diagnosis.

Blood, body parts and secretions have been used within creative and spiritual practices since time immemorial, although AIDS has changed the attitude of society towards such work. Your art was groundbreaking, in my opinion, in utilizing atavistic and primal resources to confront contemporary issues. Is it possible that you have set a trend to use the same medium purely as money making technique? How would you feel about that?

There could be no doubt that I knew using my AIDS-tainted blood to paint with would be a controversial, but I never thought about it as a money making technique. There is never a guarantee that artwork is going to sell and especially for the first series in 1995, I never thought anyone would buy them. And even now their money making ability is sporadic at best. I think their ability to provoke thought, strike conversation and force the viewer into a somewhat uncomfortable place is the ultimate reward for me. If it sells or not becomes irrelevant.

I never decided to be an artist, I just always was, but I did decide I never wanted to rely on it as a sole source of income. I felt that if I had to rely on it, I'd be more likely to give in to pressure to paint or create what would make money. So I have always maintained a "full-time day" job. For the past fifteen years I've maintained a "day job" as a social worker and now a program manager of social service programs, ironically, that assist low income persons and those with HIV/AIDS.

Interview with Steed Taylor

Born in North Carolina and educated at the University of North Carolina, American University and the Skowhegan School for Painting and Sculpture, Steed Taylor's (steed@steedtaylor.com) art practice includes public art projects as well as work for galleries. His art has been discussed in publications as varied as *Art in America* to *Vibe Magazine* and he is featured in *Playboy Magazine Jan/Feb 2010 Issue, 'The New Modern Art'*.

Were you an artist before your diagnosis as being HIV positive?
Yes. I was 24 or 25 when I was diagnosed in 1984 or 1985. I had finished my undergraduate studies, which were in creative writing and studio art concentrating on printmaking.

How did the diagnosis change your creative approach?
At first I avoided putting my diagnosis and information about that part of my life into my art. When my test came back positive, the doctor told me I would die within 2 years. Friends and acquaintances were dying all around me; it was a very difficult time. Although I was avoiding putting this into my art, it was seeping in, so I eventually embraced it and did several self-portraits. Eventually, longing and loss became a major theme in my artwork.

Why did you feel the need to work with blood?
I am not really sure. I thought about doing the blood prints for a few

years before I did the first one. I wanted to get back in touch with printmaking and this was a way to do it without finding a press or print studio to use and it combined the focus of my work. I had become friends with the artist Copy Berg, who had an aspect of physical endurance/pain management in his art practice as well as seeing a show by Bob Flanagan who used his cystic fibrosis the same way. The idea really stuck with me and I kept mulling it over for quite a while. I had been in a lot of emotional pain from dealing with so much death and loss that the cathartic aspect of controlled bleeding/controlled pain was appealing.

Was there anything in your religious or cultural make up that links in with this type of work?

I was raised a Baptist and was somewhat religious as a child. After my diagnosis, I became very spiritual which helped me get a grip on what was happening to me, helped me understand and accept my place in the world and got me to see my life as part of something bigger. So yes, the importance of blood was very much part of my awareness, both as something sacred and as tool of infection and doom.

Who does the cutting?

I do the cuttings using a scalpel, sometimes drawing the design on the skin.

Who do you cut?

Almost all of the people have been friends of mine or friends of friends. Also, because many of my friends are HIV+, most of the blood prints are made with HIV+ blood.

Do you do the cutting in a mundane environment or do you ritualise it?

Before the cutting, we would have talked about what is involved in the entire process, decided on a design and placement of the cutting.

Once I start cutting, it can be pretty intense, physically and emotionally, for the person getting cut which causes a kind of bond to form between us which isn't exactly ritualized but more of a supportive combined effort. The person knows I need to keep cutting so I can finish the design while the blood is still flowing so I can make the prints.

Does the cutting leave scars?

It varies. Most of the time, the cuttings heal rather quickly leaving very little mark. Other times, thin white lines remain after the cuttings heal. Rarely scars remain. The cutting that spelled out *Merry Christmas* which I did for a holiday theme show in 2007 formed visible scars but they are getting lighter and lighter over time. Another time, the person wanted the scars to remain so I rubbed charcoal into them.

Is the process mood altering?

Yes it is. I don't exactly think of it that way but it is very intimate, awareness of time shifts, giving and accepting pain are transcended. We are working together to get a desired goal, but it actually happens pretty quickly.

Has the audience reaction been what you expected, and is that attitude changing?

I have shown this work only twice, once in Charlotte, NC and one piece in 2007. It was not well accepted either time. Most people don't take to it and don't want to know more about it.

Quite a few of the HIV positive artists I have spoken to have long outlived their expected prognosis and the peers who were diagnosed at a similar time. Obviously there may be mundane reasons for this; however do you think it is possible that the act of creative and spiritual expression holds a measure of healing in it?

Definitely. I think creative and spiritual expression can be healing. I think they can help bring about physical wellness; and, I think they help you become quiet and centred, help you get to a state of grace, so you can face what life has given you even if physical wellness is not possible.

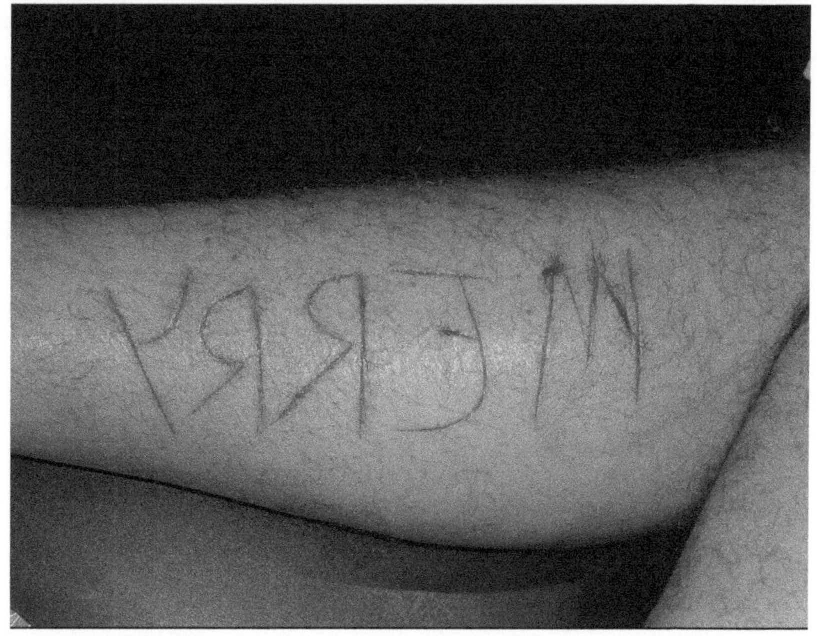

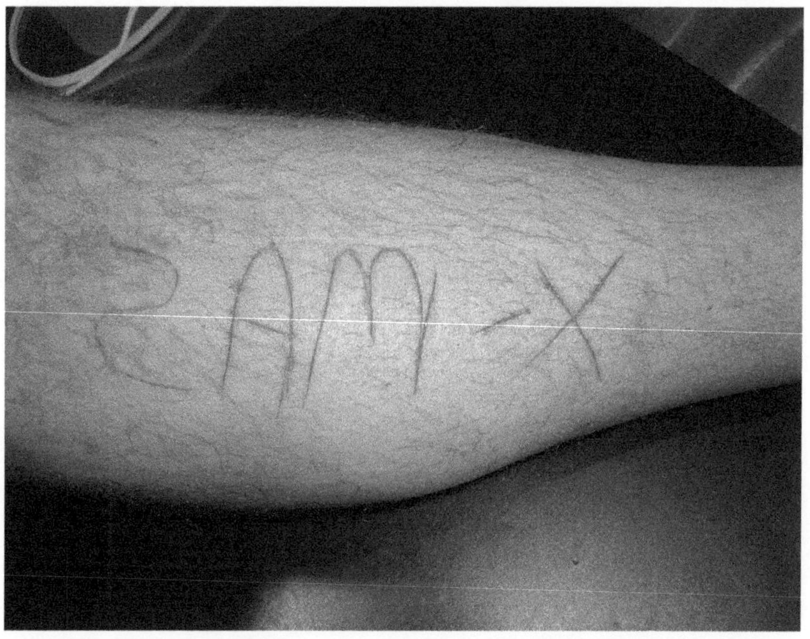

'Blood Prints' by Steed Taylor

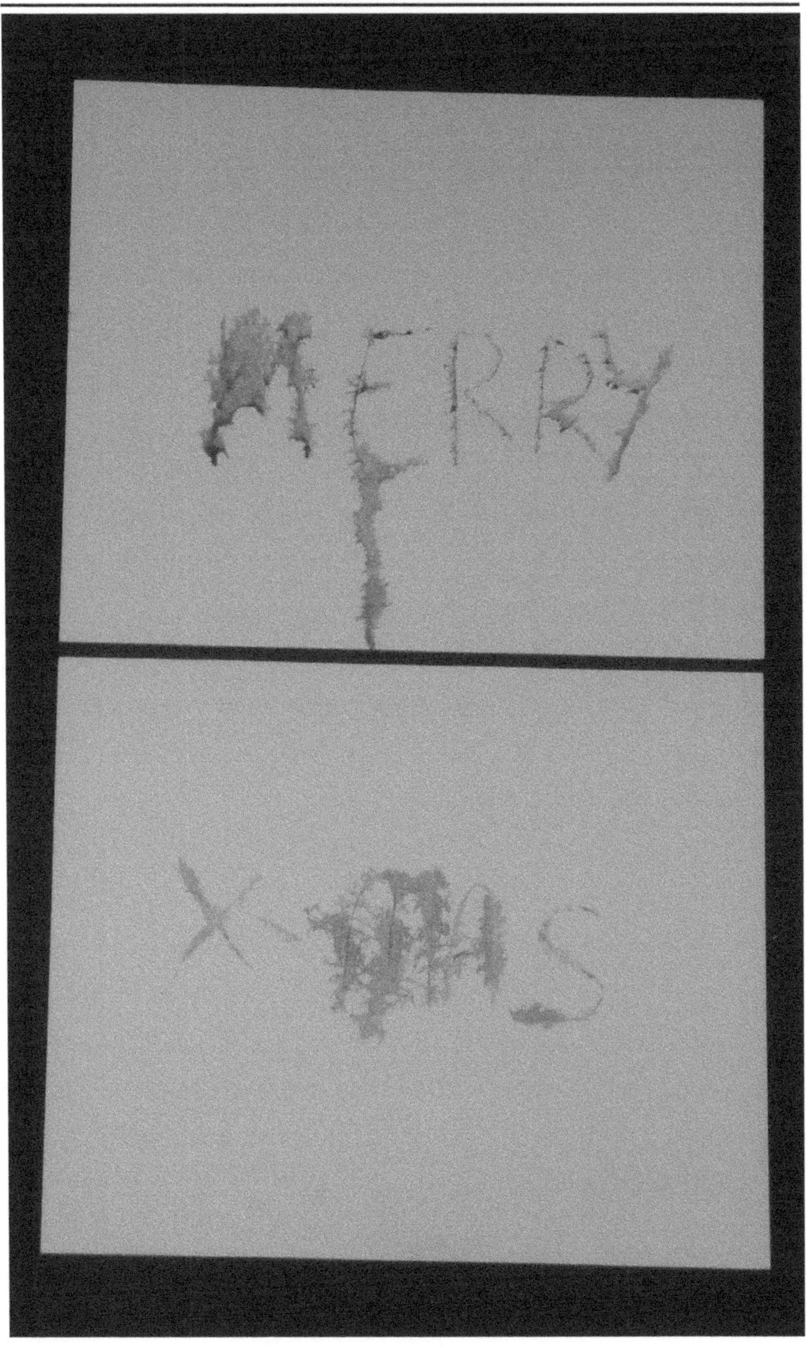

'Blood Print' by Steed Taylor

Interview with Mishlen Linden

Mishlen Linden (http://www.mishlenlinden.com/) is a magickian, musician, artist and writer and the author of the definitive *Typhonian Terotomas* which Kenneth Grant considered to be 'too dangerous to publish'. She has been a practising Tibetan Buddhist for over 15 years.

Many years ago Mishlen was a great help to me when I was doing research into menstruation and we bonded over our shared use of bones and road kill in our respective art work. As someone who works with animal remnants in her art and as a committed Tibetan Buddhist with a training in Western Esoteric Traditions I believe Mishlen has valuable insights into the use of blood in art and spirituality.

How do you perceive 'blood'?

In a Kabbalistic framework, I would have to say Kether is the element of air, and it is blood that controls our inner bodies to breathe. Therefore, I see blood as the medium of Grace, bringing air to the cells it reaches. When the breath stops, the heart stops. When the heart stops, breath stops. These two organs are linked to each other by blood, by air.

Do you believe there is a difference between venous and menstrual blood?

Yes. Menstrual blood is cast forth from the body at regular intervals, and I believe it carries a greater risk of drawing the beings, called larvae, that are drawn to such blood, feed off it, and then move into yourself. This open portal invites such beings to come and stay. This is undesirable, to say the least. Perhaps this is why a great many religious and spiritual practices are put aside during menstruation. Venous blood, however, is given once, and does not create a passageway into the body, but rather, can hover around it or - more usefully - that which is anointed by it.

When I was doing my own work that using different blood types in context of sacrifice I found I had more problems with venous blood. When I fed menstrual blood to creatures I had created or connected with from other realms it proved to be far less problematic than feeding them venous blood which seemed to generate an appetite for more! Do you have any experiences or opinion of the above?

I had answered this one, but upon thinking on it more deeply, I've changed my mind! I think its dependent upon the type of spirit you are working with. This is why when I was down in the Yucatan (Mexico, Mayan), I became ill after a visit to one of their sacrificial cenotes, or deep pools formed by karst earth and used as sacrificial grounds. It was assumed that I had an internal parasite (as I did, but not the kind they were looking for). When I returned home, I was treated for such, without success. The medical profession were angry, as if it was my fault. But before they gave up, they took many blood draws from me, and oddly, I felt better for a while after they had done it.

Still, I went into a slow decline. In time, I was whittled down to a skeletal appearance at 98 lbs, and got around by crawling, for I had no energy to walk upright. I gave away my magickal tools, and prepared to die.

There was a phone call. A woman I knew who lived in the Blueridge Mountains knew a man who had studied under a Cherokee shaman, and was known for his miraculous cures. I had nothing to lose. If he couldn't help, he would tell you straight out, which increased my respect of him. He looked at me and said he wondered how I was still alive (it was because my magickal friends would gather weekly around me and give me life force). Then he looked at a clear quartz crystal I wore around my neck (I SWEAR, this was before the New Age crystal rage). I had been wearing it for several years. He took it off, made some passes over it, and left the room. I'll never know what he did. When he came back into the room, he declared that it had a vitality eating spirit housed in it and asked where I had gone lately..of course, it was to the cenote', where sacrifices are still made. It made sense. He gave it back to me and said it was now cleansed. He became very serious. From now on, he said, I would get better. He also recommended that I wear coloured stones instead of quartz because 'it can pick up anything, being clear'. Needless to say, I did not put it on again...rather, I rid myself of it.

I got better, slowly. I lived at the top of a mountain that had a path through a beautiful forest, and a tame deer that would follow me home. There was a big waterfall and rocks to lie on and bathe in the sun. It took a year to recover, but I did.

The deer didn't learn to fear humans, but I learned to fear - in a healthy way - the astral larvae that could leach onto life-force that glowed brightly-like those of many magickans who strengthened their astral bodies and made them clearer to such. One of the dangers of our occupation, I'm afraid.

Why couldn't I have seen it for myself? Why hadn't my magickal friends seen it? I think the creature had wound itself through me and through my aura, and it became indistinguishable from it. I had had dreams of Chinese serpent-type dragons battling with me. I did not take them literally. I should have. I relate this to show how easily blood working can become dangerous.

Without a controlled ritual, blood is a power magnet. What you want to connect to is up to you. A friend of mine ate her menstrual blood as the Oroboros eats its own tail. I create spirits, but they require a constant amount of nourishment that I am rarely able to get into the habit of feeding, and they dissolve back into the aethers until I remember to feed them again.

I think, personally, that the plasm-protoplasm - is the vital essence of the blood we are using. Mana, amrita, ashe', a thousand different words used in a thousand different cultures.

I have passed my time of moon-bleeding - now the bloodshed must come from my heart. I read that once, it seems true now. So perhaps there are times for both.

An aside: in the process and ritual of killing and eating meat, from a Buddhist perspective which I work with now, it is said that eating meat will combine your karma with the karma of the animals and that will leave you 'heavier'.

How you feel about art that utilizes blood in some way?

As one of the essences-kalas of the body, I believe it gives great power to a piece. It also creates a lasting bond. I use spit in my art for the same reason. Both contain your DNA, and what that DNA writes, so is the piece inscribed.

Have you ever used blood in your artwork?

I sculpt using all the elements - wood, bone, stone and feathers. Why would I stop there? Some pieces require it of me, others do not. In Tibetan Buddhism, the deities, as it were, can be divided into peaceful Buddha's and wrathful protectors. Those that are wrathful are given offerings suited to their natures - blood, meat, alcohol, a very strong tea that acts like ephedrine. This, I think, is the ground floor from which magick is based-that one gives offerings 'according to its nature'.

With the evolution of your spirituality, has there been an accompanying change in your attitude towards the use of blood in art and ritual?

I feel free to use my own blood, but not another's without permission and full disclosure of the process of the rite. As I learn more, I use more discretion. If it is not necessary, I don't use it.

You use bones, fossils and other remnant of the living in your art. Why?

Each gives a part of its innate power to the whole. Make a temple to a god, and he will come and indwell it. This is true of all magick's, including the lesser spirits, whose houses I make.

Does working in these mediums change you in any way?
My icons are created in a frenzy of joy, just as sex creates a body. We all do this. My perspective is only a little bit larger. We are ALL creators. We are all gods of our tiny multiverses.

Do you think that modern morality's suppression of blood rites in religious ritual has created a spiritual loss or left a gap that has not been filled?
Modern suppression of blood rites . . . in religious ceremony... Ah, that one gives me a chance to sound off!!!

Repression??!! Not at all!! Now our ritual takes the form of mindless giving of the Will within oneself to a country and the country sends you to war, and if that's not a bloody sacrifice, I don't know what is!!!! That mindless country's song, it's rituals of uniform and acting on a herd instinct; the orders and commands-what is that if not ritual?

Blood sacrifice is alive and well, and growing, now that we can fly from one part of the global village to another. It began as land grabbing. It progressed to war, and it is our own flesh that we see on the plate before us.

Mortification

> 'The term mortification drives from the Latin word mortificare (to put to death) ... some practices of mortification seem intended to symbolically assimilate the initiate into a deathlike condition that is to precede an initiatory rebirth.' Mircea Eliade

Using body mortifications and modifications as a conscious tool to explore spirituality and trance, came relatively late to me.

In my adolescence, as was fitting for that era, I had the usual amount of piercings (i.e. more than everyone else) to mark me out as a member of a counter culture.

When I was unhappy or very wasted I would on occasion burn myself with a cigarette or cut myself with a razor.

The cutting and burning was neither an attempt to hurt or destroy myself nor was it to mark me out as being hard or tough. It actually was a means of anchoring me to a mundane and conventional reality.

I had several stints in psychiatric institutions where I saw heart breaking cases of self mutilation. People who had cut their arms or faces to oblivion, and one woman who sliced her wrists so badly that one of her hands needed to be amputated.

I've found it interesting in recent years to see people proudly display their scars and burnings, not as a mark of abberation but as a mark of belonging or initiation.

Reading tomes such as Favazza's *Bodies Under Siege: Self Mutilation and Body Modification in Culture and Psychiatry*, what strikes me first is how the author refuses to categorise the modern primitive movement as pathological. What also struck me was the sense of the loneliness and isolation that can be part of self harming.

Feelings of alienation from society and your own body seems to tap into some collective unconscious knowledge that the cutting of your body, and the letting of blood can be used as a way to go into, or outside oneself; as a means of spiritual expression and for marking a rite of passage.

Favazza posits at several points in his book that self harm is actually an instinctively practiced survival technique; sacrificing part of yourself for the greater good of the whole.

I'm not denying that there are some very ill people in contemporary western society who hurt themselves as part of their illness, but there are also people who do this because this is who they are and how they operate. Finding a place for this expression, finding peers and an accompanying spirituality takes away something that could be considered madness and makes it personal expression; albeit one that is not accepted easily within western culture.

Raven Kaldera author of *Dark Moon Rising: Pagan BDSM and the Ordeal Path* describes himself and his sexuality in terms of being a 'sick fuck' but goes on to describe how through the knowledge and acceptance of who and what he is he has found a place for himself as a shaman and ordeal master and with it a responsibility.

In Adam Phillips book *On Flirtation*, Phillips comments that psychoanalysis 'unavoidably promotes and institutionalizes the idea of an exemplary life'.

There are some of us who are different, who do not fit into standardised frames of of an 'exemplary life'.

I will not deny some people court the idea of not fitting into the standard mould, and the moment a certain behaviour or expression is normalised they need to move onto a more radical form of self expression. However human beings are not a homogenised mass which fall into tidy categories. There must be awareness of the contradiction of the way so called primitive societies are willing to not only make exceptions for, but actually celebrate that which is different while the more 'advanced' Western culture still strives to marginalize that which cannot be classified.

The epilogue in Favazza's book Body *Play: State of Grace or Sickness?* is written by the man considered to be the father of the modern primitive movement, Fakir Musafar.

In this Fakir describes a television talk show in which he, Favazza and Raelyn Gallina (who does cutting within the context of socialised ritual), appeared. Appearing with them is a woman who had spent years in various types of therapy for inveterate self harming.

The expression on the woman's face when she realised that there were others such as herself who were not considered to be mentally ill and were not treated as such but had found a place for their expressions, was telling in its realisation of a perhaps unnecessarily lonely and stigmatised life.

Living in the backwaters of New Zealand and travelling through Asia some 20-30 years ago there was very little contact to be had with people of similar inclinations to myself.

I do not categorise my predilections as masochistic but I definitely have always had a strong pull towards the spiritual aspects of physical mortification. However as I got older Hepatitis C and assorted other conditions (along with, sad to say, a certain vanity) mean that I do not experiment with body play in the name of pure sensation or physical decoration as I would have had been accessible when I was younger.

I remember talking to my now ex-husband in the 1980s and suggesting he get a Prince Albert piercing, and being told that I was a 'sick bitch', and when the book *Modern Primitives* came out it was to a huge fascinated Hurrah! from myself.

As a solitary practitioner there are many aspects of mortification that I've only encountered through reading and conversation and I've learned a lot about myself from what has shocked me.

Truth to tell the darkest places I have been in my research for this book has not been while looking at ritualised eye stitching or brandings, or kitchen table castrations in trendy New York art galleries; it has been reading the psychiatric tomes and the details of the lonely suffering of clinically treated 'self harmer'.

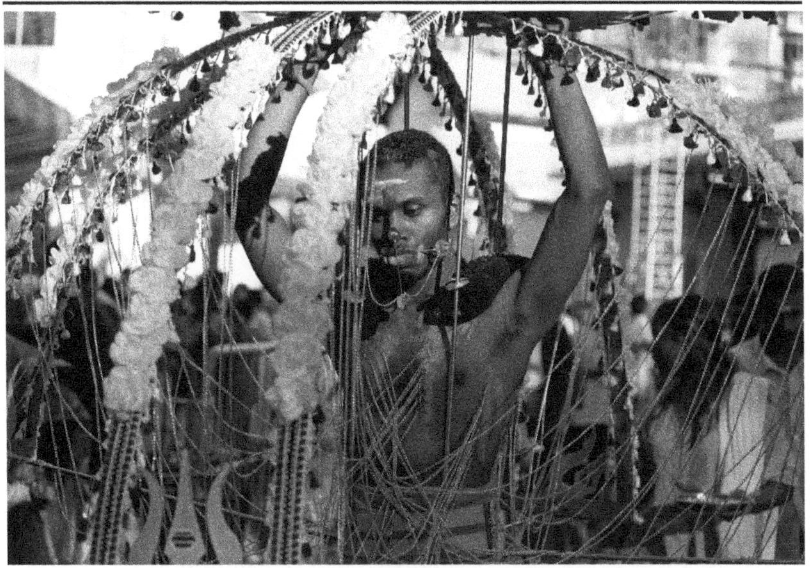

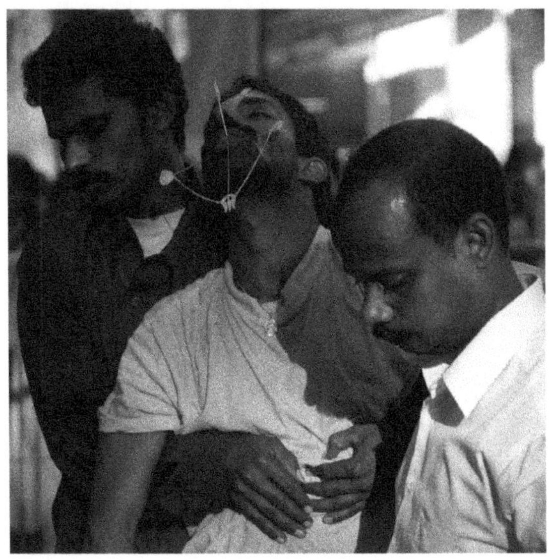

'Thaipusam Celebrations, Singapore.' Images by Ian Selbie

Personal

As with much of my magickal work I did not start experimenting with the spiritually directed applications of tattooing, piercing and scarification until I was in my early thirties.

As I mentioned in the introduction to this section I utilised these techniques in the year's prior but there was no conscious direction in my actions.

Rather there was a flailing around and an attempt to grasp at something that was lurking on the proverbial edge of my consciousness but which I couldn't fully comprehend.

The last time I deliberately injured myself outside context of magickal application was also the time that I realised what I was doing and why.

I was living in a dry house, some 15 years ago and I was so angry I started to disassociate from my body with fear of the power of my rage.

I burned my ankles as a distraction from my anger and as a way to reconnect with my body. Being an analytical person I thought afterwards about what I had been doing.

I eventually realised that deliberately caused localised pain comes with an intensity that could be used as either a distraction or as a means of focusing.

Musing on the power of my own directed rage I realised therein lay a potential for very powerful magickal tool.

I filed away this revelation, together with the reasons for my actions. I never found the need to self harm again either as a distraction from fears of personal power, or as punishment for feelings of vulnerability.

Sometime after this I decided to decorate my body with a ritualised pierce of tattoo work. This tattoo was to be placed at the base of my spine thus reclaiming my body post rape and abuse and creating a barrier against further assaults (as Mexican prison inmates are tattooed with an image of Our Lady of Guadalupe on their backs for protection), as well as acting as a marker of a new phase of existence. This led to a series of other tattoos that mapped out in my terms who I was, and where I wished to go; both in a spiritual and worldly context.

Finding a skilled tattoo artist who is also willing to work in a spiritual and ritualised manner was no easy task and when I did come across a person who was willing to tattoo under these conditions, I had almost all my body work performed by him.

At one stage however we had a falling out and it took seven years before I could locate the right person to finish a specific piece of body work.

Eventually I found a tattooist with similar spiritual inclinations to myself. During the previous work I had done I had become aware of the dynamic of power and responsibility that a tattoo artist holds over his client as well as a sexual element that can be present, and I decided to experiment with these concepts.

The second tattooist I found worked in the traditional Japanese manner called irezumi which doesn't utilise the standard Western tattoo gun but is hand applied, so we were able to explore initiatory and transitional rites that the completion of this tattoo symbolised, and combine them with a period of sexual magickal ritual.

This had enormous effect on both my own and the artist's lives which is what we had aimed for.

I have utilised scarification to positive and transformational purpose as well.

I created a sigil of Shiva/Shakti conjoined and had my lover cut this into my upper right arm to create within me, rather than merely symbolise, the joining of masculine and feminine energies for progressive change.

In this sort of situation the focus on the pain of each cut trains the mind to 'feel' the embedding of intent onto every level. As healing occurs and the scab forms and drops away the intent is forgotten because it becomes simply a part of who you are.

Piercing is something which I have used on occasion, sometimes for fun or sexual purposes and sometimes as a focus on a specific part of the body that needs to be worked with.

There are times when I've felt that I want to 'do' something, but that a tattoo or scarification is not appropriate so I follow my intuition and this generally leads to a piercing.

The key point in all of the above is that my body is as much a part of my spirituality as my mind and my spirit.

Awareness of my physical self means that there are times where it is necessary to work on this level, just as much as it may be appropriate at other times to utilise other facets of myself.

I'm aware that there is a trickster element built into both the world within and the world without, so I retain awareness about my actions and the reasons for them, something especially necessary as such work does bear a highly addictive quality.

Interview with Steven V Mitchell

Steven V Mitchell (www.darkblackart.com) has been a tattoo artist for 25 years. Recently his medium has expanded to include sculpture and painting.

As a tattoo artist who also does piercings, I considered Steven to be someone who is a modern initiator of blood rites.

The fact that he has also worked in non Western societies which view tattoo work in a sacred context, makes Steven Mitchell's opinions all the more interesting.

How long have you been doing this work?
I've been tattooing professionally for over twenty years.

Do you consider your work as filling a role in society?
Yes. It has a long history in the West, and has always been used for marking rites of passage, social status and ranking in subcultures i.e. sailors, gang members, prostitutes: all wore different symbols to mark rank or their personal rights within their group.

These symbols differ from group to group and generally relate to what that group does; for example, a merchant sailor would have a swallow tattoo on his chest to show that he has crossed the International Date Line on a voyage, and then he would have a second one done when he crossed it a second time.

These would show that he had sailed around the world and that he had experience.

The tattoos were traditionally done on the chest, but they migrated to the hands [we have all seen swallows on the hands]; because, when a ship was taking on sailors for work they could quickly see who had experience by looking at their hands. The tattoo work was their C.V.

This is just one example of tattooing in the West. It is not that different to a Huron tribal member, marking himself in a permanent way to show that he was a brave and had mastered a skill, or undertaken a rite of passage.

Do you think that modern Western Society views Tattooing and piercing in a different way than other cultures that you have worked within?

Superficially yes, it is perceived as visual body art, and fashion. However in most of the indigenous cultures I have worked with, they don't consider it so much decoration, but in a more holistic way.

They understand the aspects of rites of passage; empowerment through embodying a symbol's spirit into the body, mind and soul, with a mystical application. This was always the tattooist or medicine man's work in a tribal community. An example is women in the west getting tattooed on the sacrum [lower back] is very popular today, porn stars, and pop stars can all be seen with this mark.

In my experience, tattooing in this area does unlock a lot of root power [sexual power] in a woman.

I'm not so sure that all the western women who get tattooed in this place know why they get the tattoo there, but for sure they all are a lot happier after!

They normally say that they have seen their idols on the TV with a tattoo on the lower back and they then want one [fashion]. They follow these idols as they are seen and worshiped as gods in our culture, and copy to try to attain their heights. This is a kind of twist on religious tattooing or idol worship

This is not so different than it's always been in human society; it's just coming through in a new wave. It is human nature to want to be as great as your idol.

Do you believe that those who get tattoo or piercing work done have a subconscious pull towards the specific design they choose, something deeper and more primal than simply a whim or desire to decorate themselves?

The driving need for tattoo work in the west is deep unconscious and primal, most people don't understand this when they first walk into a tattoo studio.

The body work they choose to get done will make a statement about who they are and where they have come from. It can heal and protect them on a new path. Without exception when talking to a client they are going through a rite of passage,

Some people may well come into my studio and ask for a tattoo because a friend of theirs has one or they have seen it on TV, but most of the time on further questioning , I will discover that they are unconsciously marking a symbolic rite, or empowering themselves in a magical way.

The placement is important. I often see the placement they choose is not only for decorative reasons. They will place a symbol on a part of their body that is out of balance, or where they need to tap into a meridian permanently.

People unconsciously know where they need to be tattooed; they just can't tell you why. They just know from deep down within themselves: in the West this is the norm, it's deep, primal and instinctive.

Does tattoo and piercing work effect a change in consciousness, if so is this temporary or permanent?

Yes, in the process of tattooing, an altered state of consciousness is achieved. This is very important part; it's part of the magical process. I will try to explain this.

It's only temporary while it is being applied, then you return to day to day consciousness. You can't go through life in a permanent altered state of consciousness, as you are not going to function too well in the office the next day!!! [This is ok if you are a tribal shaman who needs to be out there all the time, but most of us don't have that job].

Most of us would have experienced the flash of 'Eureka!' an awakening, then in time it's forgotten and we go back to the office and carry on with our lives.

However at key points in our lives, we all need to get to 'Eureka!' [A spiritual awakening] to bring about permanent change/healing/or acceptance of change.

The tattoo blood rite does this perfectly in many ways, you experience the mystical in an altered state while being tattooed but you have a permanent mark, an empowering symbol, as a key back to that point in your life.

You make that moment in time last forever as you integrate it into yourself. The mark is permanent, so the rite of passage also becomes permanent. A permanent 'Eureka!' empowerment, or transition.

This is tattoo-works magical power; it bridges consciousness, and time. You can return to the office job in day to day life, but you have a tattoo that is a key back to that moment in time of 'Eureka!' and you will integrate the change into your life, with it permanently in place on all levels of consciousness.

There is a process of total surrender to the ritual passage in the West that is similar to indigenous cultures; we all have to show up and go through it to come out the other side. You walk into a tattoo studio, and come out different!!!! In what way different is as individual as the person, or symbol choosen.

In summary the change in consciousness is temporary, but the tattoo is permanent. This is in affect a magical, permanent bridge back to the moment or change in consciousness ['Eureka!']

The symbol that is tattooed defines the rite of passage and keys the symbolic power permanently into the person [so if you tattoo a bear on a guy, he will always embody that spirit].

There is also an interesting yin/yang to tattooing.

Some people need to bring out a symbol from the inside of themselves for empowerment, and some people need to bring a symbol from spirits outside to empower themselves!!!

Some of my research suggested that anyone who works as a tattoo artist or as a piercer (and is any good) is a sadist.

Yes I agree in principle, although I'm not so sure that everyone who works in the tattoo and piercing field is aware of this!!!!!!! or would agree with the word 'sadist'. Anyone who is good at body art, will be able, with compassion and an understanding of the higher purpose of the client, to push them physically beyond their normal boundaries. It is a relationship between client and tattooist that has deep trust, and the client surrenders to the artist's needle, and in that relationship a transformation is achieved. It is a little like the relationship between the sadist and the masochist ... but there is an end result that is called art; a lasting memory in and on the body.

That is interesting, especially in the light of Raven Kaldera's musings in his *Dark Moon Rising: Pagan BDSM and the Ordeal*

***Path*. In this Raven puts forward the theory that care-fully applied pain in a ritualised context is part of an Initiator path, as shown in such ceremonies as the Lakota Sun Dance, the Hindu Kavadi ceremony and so on. In this particular path the 'top' or person running the interaction has to be 'skilled, knowledge, respectful and compassionate, and intensely love hurting some real bad.' How have the attitudes towards body work changed with the advent of HIV and HCV?**

The health department have become tighter, [which is a good thing] and in fact it has helped people accept tattooing in the West, as it now cleaner and nicer, a bit like visiting the dentist. You can still have a mystical experience with clean sterile equipment.

I like my studio to be as clean as an operating theatre but feel as mystical as an opium den/bordello.

The best of both worlds!

Financial and Creative gain aside are there any other benefits for you in doing this work?

Yes, I feel the most rewarding part of the work has been my own learning of how life truly is, and how the mystical works.

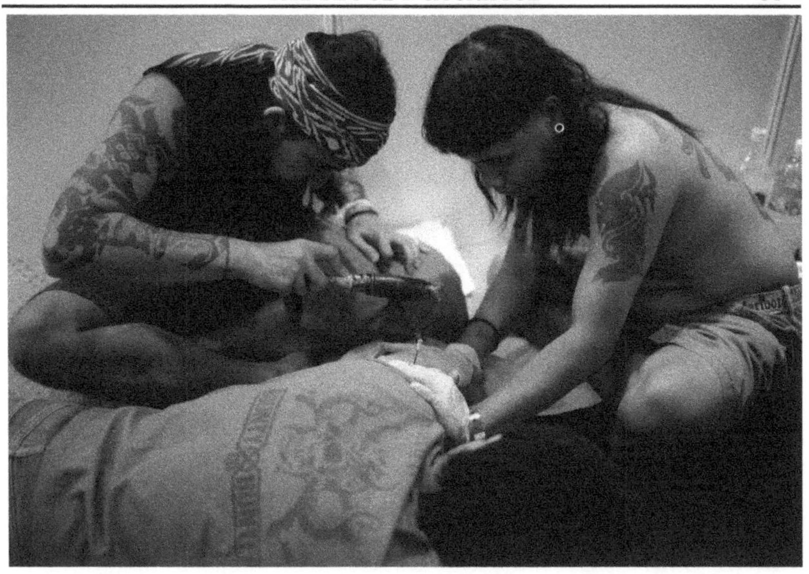

Traditional Borneo Tattoo Artists. Image by Ian Selbie.

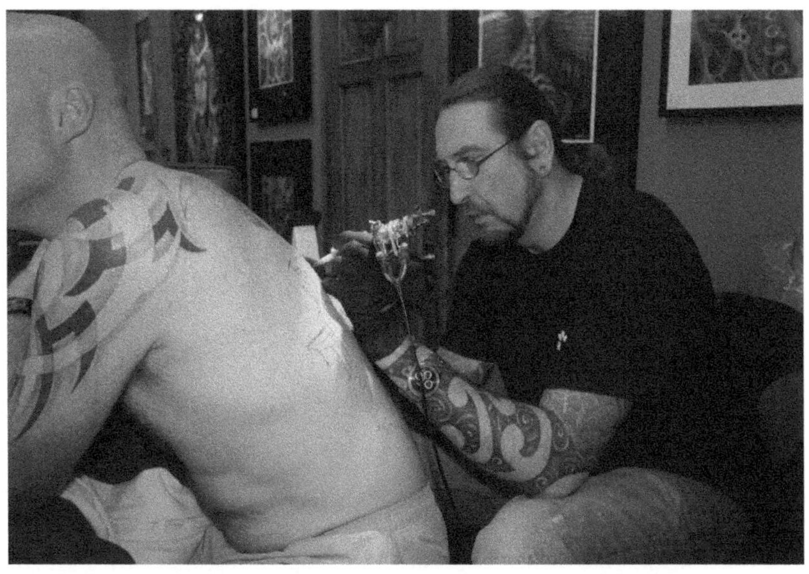

Steven V Michell working. Photograph by Jolanta Kristapaviciene.

Interview with Peter Grey

Peter Grey is a devotee of Babalon, author of *The Red Goddess* and co-founder of *Scarlet Imprint Occult and Esoteric Publishing*. He is an exponent of the antinomian and libertarian strand of the Western Magical Tradition. His work comes out of physical praxis as a student of ninjutsu, a snowboarder, free-ride mountain biker and surfer. His path is one of Ordeal, Ecstasy, and Love.

As my research is primarily focused on experiential contemporary spirituality it was necessary to look at the Modern Primitives; a movement which Roland Loomis or Fakir Musafar is considered to be the father of.

Knowing that Peter Grey uses blood in his devotional practice and that he has done workshops with Fakir, promised that my interview with him would provide insight and illumination and perhaps some identification on my part.

Peter, cutting, suspension rituals and the use of blood are all used as part of your spiritual practice. Why do you do this? Where does the performance of these acts take you and are the results consistent?

Blood is what Babalon has called 'the final solution'. Although the sacrifice of sex is vital in working with Her*; it is blood which seals the pact. The oath of the devotee is to pour every drop of blood into Her cup. By making the blood sacrifice you bind yourself to this course of action. This is particularly relevant when considering Her as a Goddess of Love and War. The awareness of a world beneath the skin and the surrendering to the act of penetration with blade or needle is a necessary transgression for the male devotee.

Modern man divorced from the experience of war is not used to bleeding, so the act of giving blood reconnects us with the reality of our mortality. Cut me, and I bleed. I grew up in a medical family. I also have dangerous pursuits which lead to me being bloodied, both in martial arts and free sports. I am no stranger to my body. However, I have a strong haemophobic response which makes the act of blood letting a difficult and arduous task. Offering venous blood does not carry an erotic charge for me.

I have written about and advocate the use of flesh pulls, suspension and cutting as a core part of magical practice. These essays can be found in the *TOPY Body Modification Grimoire* and in both *The Red Goddess* and *Devoted.* On a less dramatic level, I always draw blood when I work with roses (using the thorns) and pay careful attention to when and why I receive cuts.

The results of these offerings are evident in my Work and my connection with Babalon.

---

* Certain words capitalized throughout at Peter Grey's request.

You said that, 'The oath of the devotee (to Babalon) is to pour every drop of blood into Her cup.' and '...the surrende`ring to the act of penetration with blade or needle is a necessary transgression for the male devotee.' Do female devotees of Babalon work with blood in the same manner or is her worship individual, rather than gender, specific?

Thankfully there is no orthodoxy, and we hope that there never will be in terms of how to work with Babalon. All work is individual, so rather than being gender specific, blood work is personal. I write from my own experience and believe that it is more honest to talk about what I do rather than imposing my ideas on the whole gorgeous panoply of human sexuality. For the female devotee the ritual drinking of a partner's venous blood in identification with Babalon is one approach. In my opinion the male magician should be ritually penetrated, especially if he is heterosexual, as part of his Babalon devotion. We can see this in Crowley's act of being ritually sodomised by Victor Neuberg during his exploration of the Enochian Aethyrs. It does not have to be penetration through anal sex, another example of this would be the subincision practice of tribal peoples. This is one of the reasons behind my own genital and nipple piercings. In identifying with the seven headed Beast, the magician needs to cultivate all the planetary energies. This aspect of the work comes under the auspices of Venus.

You mentioned that you had a 'strong haemophobic response which makes the act of blood letting a difficult and arduous task.' This statement really interests me, perhaps because it's suggestive of one of the cores of my own practice: that of confrontation and reversal, be this confrontation and reversal

of ideologies, beliefs or fears. Would you be able to elaborate more on what you mean please?

The process of blood-letting often makes me physically retch, sweat, shake, fall to my knees. I have a very strong aversion to edges, needles and the sight of blood, even watching horror films can make me extremely ill. My reactions vary, as I do bleed frequently and have held together friends when they have been badly cut up in accidents. When I taste blood in sparring it simply fires my adrenals. If I found ritual blood work easy, then it would lose that crucial element of confrontation and transgression. It would also not be a sacrifice, as it would hold no value if it was easily given. The ritual crucible of willed bloodletting is one of the places where I forge myself. I seek these confrontations with myself, and She demands them.

Looking at you, and making a surface judgement I would never consider you to be the type of person who be drawn towards the 'modern primitive' movement or its associative elements. With no obvious tattoos or piercings you defy the standard image of someone who might have an interest in body play, or ritualised self mortification. Why have you affected no outward display of your interests?

I have no desire to display membership of any group or subculture, which seems to be limiting behaviour, simply substituting one set of values for another. I prefer to be fluid. The inherent conservatism of seeking after a group identity shows a lack of self rather than having found who you are. This is as rife in the body modification community as elsewhere. This is not a criticism of those who choose to be visibly modified. There are also many modifications which do not suit my physical practices and would be detrimental rather than enhancements.

Would you be able to say what sort of modifications these are and why they would be detrimental for you?

Surface and facial piercings would be torn out in martial training. Subdermal implants whether horns or silicon or steel present areas of vulnerability to impacts. For full-contact living, robust piercings and removable earrings are essential.

Although you seem quite a bit younger than me you still don't appear to be of the generation that information about these things was easily accessible unless you made a very deliberate effort to hunt them out.

Genesis P-Orridge has always been an inspiration. Like most others I have a tattered copy of the ReSearch *Modern Primitives* book which both appalled and fascinated me. Spending time in Brighton, the remnants of TOPY and the original Wildcat exerted a real pull on me. With its queer culture and history of transgressive pleasures it was the first place in the UK which really took to the needle. It still has a markedly high level of tattooists and aware piercers. I have always hunted after forbidden knowledge and practices this is simply part of that trajectory.

Why did you decide to do a workshop with Fakir?

The approach of Fakir is that bodyplay is spiritual. The stunning black and white photographs which document his coming of age in a basement in the mid-west, impaled on hooks, corseted or clothes pegged have a beatific quality to them. Fakir is almost alone in taking the spiritual approach rather than one of thrill-seeking and sensationalism. I took part in a flesh pull rite with Fakir because he is the father of the movement, in a sense this was shaktipat, in another, I was looking to him to understand how I could develop my own ritual practice and in particular work with initiating others into it.

Is your practise sexual, spiritual or sensationalist at its core?
I make no distinction between the spiritual and sexual. I would not describe my work as sensationalist. Perhaps it would be better to call is sensation-seeking, that is, the exploration of the limits and possibilities of the body.

Over the years I have found with say, ritual use of hallucinogenics you reach a point where the drug shows you where you can go, and often you are eventually able to reach that place without it. Is that the case with your experience of body play?
In theory all previously accessed states can be re-accessed. I can certainly do that with some threshold and altered states, however not with the more powerful psychedelic or entheogenic encounters. Body play needs repetition, as with shamanism, it is a series of learned techniques. Banging a drum once does not make you a drummer. As with Ayahuasca, keep taking the medicine. I have so much more to learn, in particular with hook pulling which seems to me the most powerful technique in that it allows you duration and volume control rather than the all-or-nothing of suspension. The example of the Plains Indians and their reverence for the Sundance bears this out.

One thing I have mused on is with the rise in awareness and

numbers interested and involved in the practices that fall under the umbrella of the term 'modern primitives', there is a taking away of the loneliness and perhaps also the need of labelling as clinically ill which these practices used to lead to. Do you have an opinion on this?

These practices can be done safely, despite their apparent physical impossibility. At its best the modification community offers clear advice on how to perform procedures and provides the ritual framework for self-knowledge. It also supports individuals who would otherwise be marginalised. The flipside is that it can create a feeling that unless you have the check list of micro-dermal, tongue split, subincision or whatever, then you do not belong. There are few ritually aware people in the industry and many hacks and fashion victims. Modification to reclaim and empower the body is possible, and it is not for me to say whether a decision to brand, or nullify, or scarify, or implant, is a sign of clinical illness. Each individual is responsible for their actions. Each artist must also accept their responsibility in working with their client to ensure that they get the desired outcome, or refuse to do the procedure.

Certainly there is an endorphin release which cutting gives that can make this a form of self-medication, an attempt to balance the body through bloodletting. I see nothing wrong with this: if you love your scars. If it is done with Love. We are all seeking to come into balance, to discover who we are by cutting into, inserting under, or inscribing magical marks on our skins.

Sacrifice

Writing on the nature of blood sacrifice in contemporary terms has proved to be incredibly difficult for me.

It would have been easier if I had focused solely on the historical aspects of blood. I could have pondered on the landmarks in the history of Judaism, Christianity and Islam as I explored Abraham's aborted sacrifice of his son Isaac. I would recount tales of the Mayans self mortifications and bloody rituals; the Naga head hunting rites and the human sacrifice and eating of victims that was used by many archaic cultures. I may even have surmised that these rituals have been sanitised for modern moralist's greater comfort, as in the transubstantiation of the Eucharist in the Catholic mass.

However - much as I have enjoyed my research into the above past practices - my focus is on the modern spiritual experiences of blood rites in the Western world.

Using historical and recorded sources creates a distance from the subject matter, whereas looking at and experiencing a subject in real time brings with it an emotional element that can be uncomfortable, disturbing, and sometimes painful.

Sacrifice translates as 'to make sacred'. Whilst the act of sacrifice can be seen to elevate the sacrificial object into something with more status than it originally held, my own research also leads me to believe that one's personal attachment and value of the sacrificial object makes an enormous difference as to how it is received.

Rene Girard posits that sacrifice is a necessary way to diffuse an inherent violence in human nature. A violence which left unchecked becomes endemic.

He suggests that sacrifice; be it plucked from the archaic Greek pharmakos, used by primitive tribal groups or sanctioned by the modern justice system, are ways of sacrificing a lesser quantity for the greater good and of keeping harmony and order within the community and the cosmos.

Interestingly enough, Favazza, whose work I mentioned in an earlier chapter of this book had similar thoughts on sacrifice for the greater good, when he talks of patients in test studies who amputated or removed body parts as a survival technique.

If thy right eye offends thee pluck it out and cast it from thee...

Whilst I appreciate Girard's view of sacrifice being a method of achieving order in a chaotic world I find it limited.

There are other forms of sacrifice which I believe he has not acknowledged. Sacrifice in the name of cementing and confirming a relationship with a god form, sacrifice for love and for personal progression, and sacrifice in the name of establishing gender and identity.

Also there is the Islamic Thabiha and the Jewish Shechitah, the respective halal and kosher slaughter of animals for consumption as food, where the animal has its throat cut and is bled to death. These are so highly ritualised and integrated into society that it is easy to forget that they are a religously sanctioned blood sacrifice.

Blood seems to have the ability to create an excitation and frenzy with its presence. The smell of it in the slaughterhouse causes panic in living animals and when blood is used in religious ceremonies, performance art or 'action-happenings' there is invariably a strong reaction from the audience. This reaction often comes with associative behaviour which one would think was the antithesis of modern social etiquette.

Whether this is a phenomena connected to blood in its actuality or whether this is only related to the concept of blood, remains to be seen.

Qorbanot, the Jewish term for sacrifice was once considered to be a major part of their religious ritual, and included blood sacrifice. This blood sacrifice stopped with the fall of their last designated sacrificial area, their temple in Jerusalem. Qorbanot is something so vital to the completeness of their religion it is believed that it will be reinstated with the coming of their Messiah. However despite the Jews long tradition of NOT being able to practice animal sacrifice, anti Semitism was for many centuries largely based on the concept of blood libel and the false belief that Jews tortured and killed Christians to use their blood for ritual purposes.

The necessity of using blood in ritualised sacrifice is something which Louis Martinie, a priest in the New Orleans Voodoo Temple challenged. He was gracious enough to talk to me about his change in attitudes towards the role blood plays within rituals.

I use blood in my own work, however blood sacrifice of another being is not a necessary part of my practise, although I have no qualms about using road kill in my sculptures.

I fluctuate between being vegan and vegetarian but have no conflict about teaching myself to skin, eviscerate and preserve the dead, a process which I find atavistic and transformative in the way it taps into a primal aspect of self.

At one stage, many years ago, there was a great interest in an archaic sacrificial initiation ritual called 'The Toad Rite' where a living toad is killed and its bones used to make a pact with the devil. Various quarters encouraged me performing this rite, partially because no woman in contemporary times, at this point, had undergone it.

Intellectually and emotionally I felt no block at the concept of spiritually motivated animal sacrifice and believed that I was capable of performing it if the opportunity arose. However one morning I woke up to find a large, live toad sitting by my bed and I realised that I neither wanted nor needed to kill it and that my initiation lay in discovering this aspect of my nature.

I had discovered that literal sacrifice of another was not spiritually right for me, and placed the toad in the garden, where I still see him on occasion.

Personal

Menstrual blood is as fascinating as venous blood with its ambiquity, holding both creative life force and death within.

Societies could be showing their respect and awareness of this by making the menstruating woman a pariah who contaminates all that she has contact with, or the laws and traditions around this matter could simply be reflecting a patriarchal and misogynistic society.

As stated by Pliny in his *Natural History*, contact with menstrual blood turned new wine sour, crops touched by it became barren and fruit fell from trees, hives of bees died and dogs who tasted it got rabies. Such lore, combined with Old Testament teachings led to strict insistence that intercourse during menstruation was to be avoided at all cost. Any child conceived during this time was likely to be born with red hair and to contract leprosy. The mere gaze of a menstruating woman might have dire consequences: children in their cradles could be poisoned by the glance of an old woman who still had her periods, the logic being that the retention of her menses emit poisonous vapors through her eyes.

The ruling of the eight century *Penitential of Theodore* stated that menstruation was unclean and on the question whether a menstruating woman should take communion ruled that, *'Women shall not in the time of impurity enter a church or communicate, neither nuns nor laywomen; if they presume (to do this) they shall fast for three weeks.'*

The menstruating Romany woman is known as mahrime or unclean and similarly the Eritreans believe menstruation to be an illness and a woman is forced to spend the week of her period in a pit reserved for the contaminated.

Orthodox Jews believe that during 'niddah', the time of a woman's menstrual flow, a husband and wife may not touch. There are other additional restrictions in place such as

* They cannot touch (even indirectly using an intermediate object).

* They cannot handle an object at the same time.

* They cannot sit together on an object that moves (a swing etc).

* They cannot eat from the same plate.

* They cannot serve food to each other.

* They must sleep in separate beds.

* They may not engage in flirtatious behaviour.

* Although spouses must continue to dress attractively, they cannot dress provocatively.

* They should cover parts of the body that are normally uncovered only in front of their spouse.

* They should not wear perfume, cologne, etc.

Whilst these examples seem extreme, they are actually representative of widespread and standard views on the subject.

Male children in Papua New Guinea are considered to be contaminated by a woman's blood at birth and remain polluted until they are initiated into manhood. Then they go through a reenactment of their birth with an honorary male (actually a post menopausal woman) acting as the mother. Thus they are reborn without contact with a woman's blood.

This is an interesting example in that it seems to ally with the Christian belief of original sin and of a woman being the cause of this sin which only a rebirth (in the case of Christianity, a baptism) can remove.

Another interesting aspect of my research was looking at what could be considered to be a male envy of menstruation.

There are theories that the Amer-Indian sweat lodge is a male attempt to emulate the female's monthly purge.

Subincision, the splitting open of the urethra, is practiced by the Wogeo men of Papua New Guinea in emulation of the purification which women undergo during menstruation.

Subincision and supercision (where the prepuce is cut but no skin is removed) is practiced in Australia, South America, Fiji and Africa: one theory is that it is done to simulate the female genitals (Roheim

1949) this argument being enhanced by the fact that men often gash the subincised or supercised penis to draw blood during rituals.'

> *'Seeing in the female that blood originated from the vulva, what is more natural than to make it come from the analogous organ in the male'* (Montague 1946-47, p.432)

It is interesting to note that there is actually very little reference to menstrual blood being used in tribal spiritual practices, and in religions such as Santeria, which is an African Diaspora religion; women who are menstruating do not participate in ceremonies.

However Tantric and Alchemical practices do consider the menstruating woman to be essential to their practice.

The folk Tantric practices or sadhana of the Bauls of Bengal sometimes include sex with menstruating women, which are described in their songs as 'full moon at the new moon'. Occasionally this is combined with the ingestion of a drink compounded of semen, blood and bodily fluids - thus making a firm Tantric statement whilst flouting established norms and taboos.

The medieval alchemists of Europe considered that an essential ingredient for the philosopher's stone was to be found *in menstruo meretrice*, 'in the menses of a whore' and a similar idea prevailed in Tantric alchemy.

The Chinese also place great belief in the restorative qualities of

Hsien T'ien Tan Ch'ion pills of which the menstrual discharges of young and beautiful girls were the main ingredient.

While all the above is fascinating and perhaps helps give insight into the contradictory fascination of the menses, it still tends to be illustrative of the views of others so I decided to embark upon my own exploration of menstruation and its practical, experiential, spiritual and creative applications and effects.

This could be seen as a very 1960s/1970s way of reclaiming my body and perhaps it was. Magickal practice is something that encompasses every aspect of self and 'knowing myself' meant knowing how my body worked. As a woman in my 30s; looking at my menstrual cycle seemed to be an obvious starting point.

I was somewhat dissatisfied by the information I came across in my research which was too often presented by men, and occasionally women, with a not unbiased agenda.

I also found that whilst recognition and utilization of the phases of the moon and their different influences is a norm in most ritual practices, working with the menstrual cycle and the blood produced is not.

An interesting but I feel relevant point was presented by Paul Katzeff in his book, *Moon Madness.*

It is a known and documented fact that acts of violence increase on the full moon, however what is less known is that it is also documented that there is also a great rise in violence (but towards the self rather than towards others) at the time of the new moon.

The reason I have pointed this out is to illustrate cycles of the moon charting relationships, between yourself and the world around you.

This seemed to me to be a good reference point for my explorations: looking at different phases of the menstrual cycle and how they affect the ability to relate, both inwardly and outwardly.

To gain a wider perspective, I drew up a questionnaire which was answered by women from a variety of geographical, cultural and spiritual perspectives.

I also quizzed men about their experiences with menstrual blood and working with and around a partner's cycle.

The questionnaires and resultant in depth conversations gave me a wider view of the menstrual cycle than I may have otherwise had. It also helped inspire the obsession which I find is necessary to do such research.

As this was such a broad topic I tried to be as specific as possible, primarily dealing with the days prior to and days actual, of menstruation.

The three days prior to menstruation are potentially the greatest times of power for all types of magickal application particularly that concerned with the working with others.

What masks itself as 'PMT' in modern day parlance is actually an intense power that can be used for focused ritual. However the need for training and guidance is essential, as due to a conditioned perception of the onset of menstruation as a time of instability a tendency to delusion is possible. This could create difficulty with in-depth magickal work.

This delusion could be seen to manifest on an earthly level as a form of bodily discomfort and twisted self image which contradicts the rise in sex drive which is calling for a celebration and expression of the profound level of energy that is available.

This is an ideal time to do sexual magickal workings as the surge of power, in the right environment can carry the woman and any working partner(s) to previously inaccessible areas of exploration.

When menstruation proper starts the woman will feel a need to consolidate her own energy for the first few days. This is an ideal time for scrying, astral work, divination of every sort, meditation and personal rituals.

However I feel great care is needed at this time in work of a sexual nature if 'communing' with entities or astral manifestations. I feel that at this point in the cycle a woman becomes like a battery of sorts where she gives out energy but will have great difficulty recharging herself. Thus there is a greater risk of obsessive magickal relations and consequent drainage on the part of the female practitioner.

Aside from excessively low energy levels, in my experience and that of other women that I have talked to, an obsessive sexual relationship on an astral level can manifest as exhaustion, swollen and overly sensitive genitalia, hyper sexuality and an inability to have sexual relations on an earthly level and achieve satisfaction. Even long term practitioners with years of training may well have trouble working at this time.

At this point in the menstrual cycle the ability to travel between worlds is at its peak; however the vulnerability in this travel is greatest. I find that if this sort of work is going to be done it is necessary to access some sort of other-worldly help, pre-journey. An alternative is to have your magickal partner on hand to help ground you post traveling.

This grounding is oft as simple as being held and touched with love; the recognition of there being unconditional love existing on this plane can aid the ability to extract oneself from others.

The knowledge that there is earthing such as this can also give even greater freedom in journeying with its generation of a feeling of safety.

Blood deities are difficult to deal with whatever the source of blood and the emotional attachment that is connected with the blood in question needs always to be borne in mind.

For instance as a woman gets older her menstruation may hold with it connotations attached with the aging process or perhaps failed attempts at pregnancy that would be detrimental if not acknowledged and dealt with before any ritual commences.

If there is no awareness of these emotional attachments, the blood can act as either a magnet to related negative entities, or twist perception of that which is contacted.

It is quite normal for women in groups to unconsciously synchronize their cycles; however the ability to change the timing of the menstrual cycle seems to occur on an occult level for some women.

There are instances which show that as a woman becomes more skilled in working magickally, she may find herself bleeding out of cycle at the commencement of a ritual.

This has happened to me on several occasions when in contact with male magicians with whom I'm doing sexual magickal work and also once in a group ritual. I have also found it to occur among other long-term female practitioners.

Several women that I have talked to said that they would consciously alter the timing of the onset of their menstrual cycle so that it would coincide with the start of a particularly important ritual, as they felt it enhanced the effect of this ritual.

I'm going to make what could be considered a sweeping statement here; however it makes sense when considered in correlation with my findings.

As one's experience magickally increases so does the knowledge about your body and its potentiality. The knowledge of how powerful working within the first three days of menstruation can be may stimulate the onset of bleeding: thus making of herself the ultimate sacrifice: herself in entirety.

Another point and I'll tread very wary around this one. There does seem to be a disproportionate number of miscarriages amongst certain types of practitioner.

There are various myths surrounding pregnancy stating that a woman shouldn't practice ritual of any sort, especially group ritual, in the first three months.

On many occasions I have been told of various traditional teachings that talk of miscarriage in magickal practitioners being a possible result of participating in ritual, or, even of conceiving to those not 'of the blood' i.e. those who are not considered to be of magickal lineage.

It seems clear that the womb/uterus does react to channeled magickal connection, but whether that reaction could prove detrimental to the point of miscarriage is something I could not make a judgment on.

Menstrual blood being used with intent I find to be a very personal thing as to results. I have had debates with various practitioners over this matter, and have come to the decision, as previously mentioned, the blood holds with it various aspects and attachments that come from the owner; therefore the nature of it will be appreciated on other levels just as individually.

I personally find menstrual blood to be one of the safer fluids to use as offerings. There seems less chance of it being used as a bridge for an entity to cross to this realm to cause havoc as there is with the use of venous blood and sexual fluids.

I find it works well for drawing sigils (though I think sexual fluids work better for the actual charging of said sigil), and is excellent for scrying.

Menstrual blood also is very good to feed servitors (though I find alternation with other substances is best) and I have found that servitors fed in this manner have never (touch wood) caused me problems.

However, in my personal experience I've found that consistently 'feeding' the same substance to an entity or servitor is unwise as it can open the way to an unbalanced and obsessive relationship where control is taken from the hands of the practitioner.

The more obvious signs of this loss of control being a constant pull to contact the entity in question that overrides one's will and desire.

On a seemingly mundane but no less effective note is 'baking with intent'. A variation on 'Cakes of Light', there is nothing like a smattering of menstrual blood and focused stirring to create transformational food.

This type of food can be used in rituals, celebrations, and for creating a unified consciousness in any group, or for effecting change in one's life either in general or at a deeper level.

It is ideal to use when working with Hecate, Lilith, or feminine embodiments of deities, and also in its more well known sexual alchemical applications when mixed with semen.

It also has many traditional usages which I've found to be very effective, such as love charms and the feeding of magickal plants such as mandrake, and has also been cited as main ingredients in mediaeval potions to cause mania, idiocy and catalepsy.

There are legends amongst the Romany of women who every seven years celebrate the 'Sabba' on 'The Mountain of the Moon' to confirm their pact with the Devil by means of their menstrual blood.

Needless to say using blood of any sort holds with it, since the rise in blood borne illness, a great measure of personal responsibility and respect.

Interview with Louis Martinie

Louis Martinie is a writer, percussionist, and drummer. He is also an Honorary Member of the Louisiana State Legislature. His books include *The New Orleans Voodoo Tarot* and he is the editor for Black Moon Publishing, and has been associated with the anarchistic grouping of ritual magicians known as Bate Cabal. Martinie is an elder and priest in The New Orleans Voodoo Temple and teaches and offers confirmation in an Order of Service to the Loa that combines elements of New Orleans Voodoo with Tibetan Buddhism.

I'm so pleased that you agreed to talk to me, Louis! I've known and had great respect for your work for many years. How do you define blood within the context of your own experiences and beliefs? Is this definition just applicable to venous blood, or does it apply to menstrual blood as well?

Blood is more of a metaphysical term to me. I would identify it as a substance possessing certain necessary characteristics. Blood is a liquid, life embracing, personal substance that flows within the body of its host. Liquid means flowing or capable of flowing; life embracing means carrying the grace of life, and personal means that the entity identifies some portion the self with the blood. This way of seeing blood certainly includes menstrual blood.

Given the above understanding of blood; what constitutes blood to one entity would not be blood to another. It would be tremendously ethnocentric to think of the red stuff in us as the only form blood takes. Referenced to myself, water is not blood but water is the blood of the earth. This is particularly apparent to me on an experiential level when I'm fortunate enough to be in the presence of a stream of water spilling out from a hole or serration in the earth. There is such grace, such mystery in this. In a practical ritual sense, the loa walk a water road. I pour water out from the veve (signature/ritual drawing) creating a water road for the loa.

I had a friend who worked as a janitor. His friend was angered by a supervisor so his friend got a red ink pen and scribbled 12 pages of everything from pictures to grocery lists in the red ink and gave it to the supervisor. Also, I teach in a High School here and it is very bad form to use red ink in most any capacity. Here a red liquid carries the power of human blood and is or becomes, in a very real sense, blood.

Your question brings up other questions. For example, "Do the loa have blood?" There is an odd invulnerability to injury when one is possessed. Blood does not flow easily. I have done things that later on do not make me happy to hear about. If a body shared with the loa does not bleed easily, this may mean that the loa have a sturdier form of what we call blood.

I think one of the main reasons that I thought it was important to talk to you as part of my research is because of the work that you have done merging the beliefs of New Orleans Voodoo and Tibetan Buddhism. I'm particularly interested in how you apply this integration to Voodoo blood rites. Although New Orleans Voodoo is syncretic and a living tradition surely blood

sacrifice is an integral part of its practice, and something which cannot be changed?

Yes, Blood sacrifice is a traditional part of our core practice. It is an important part, an essential part, and I now use the blood of trees. Red palm oil is an amazing substance. Okoko introduced me to it in the early 1980s and I have yet to sound the depths of its power.

I was able to spend a year with the Tibetan refugees between 2000 and 2001 and then, after Mademoiselle Katrina, there were numerous exchanges when we ourselves refugeed to a town populated by many Tibetans.

The Tibetans and their spiritual teachers were respectful of New Orleans Voodoo and would always politely indicate that blood sacrifice created problems for the voodoosant. They referred to "karma," something I do not understand from their perspective.

Mr. Norbu, a head of the Tibetan resistance movement, would simply say, over and over and over, that all beings were at one time my mother. He repeated this till one day I had the shattering AHA! That he was speaking literally. Given an infinite number of incarnations, every animal that I sacrificed was at one point my mother. Shit! Man, I just fell out when this got through to me. My mother, Charlotte, was so very kind to me and here I was sacrificing beings that had stood as she stood to me. I was in ceremonies that used them (her) as scapegoats. I get a little sick just thinking about it. Would I kill Charlotte to save my own skin? Fuck no! I stopped my own use of animal blood.

Blood sacrifice is a continuum and I am certainly still on the continuum. Shortly after stopping using blood in rites I was drumming for a rite conducted by an African Priestess based, I believe, in Nigeria and ended up drinking blood. So who would have known what was in the calabash? The point is that for me, doing the least harm possible is a matter of degree and we are all in this together.

The Tibetan people, in the past, used animal blood in their rites. They do not practice blood rites at present and they can successfully call powerful spirits. The same could be said for the type of New Orleans Voodoo that I practice.

Mammal blood is used in our rites for a variety of purposes. It is used for the sheer grace and power it contains. It is used to feed the loa. I have found red palm oil to be effective in both of these instances. Animal are also used for scapegoating. The Tibetans, and now I, believe in the transmigration of souls. Given an infinite number of incarnations, every sentient being one encounters has at one time been your mother. It seems cowardly to transfer my sins on to another being that has been my mother. It's like if someone shot at me and I was willing to pull Charlotte in front of me as a shield.

I am sure that at one time our loa ate people. This practice is infrequent now. The loa are not that far removed from us. As our tastes change so also do their tastes change. My ritual work has a level of success without using mammal blood that is satisfactory to me. My point is to get the most benefit for myself and others while doing the least amount of harm possible

When you reached your 'Aha!' moment did you ever consider giving up voodoo completely?

No, but I did know that I had come to what to me was an important realization and that this realization might be important to other voodoosants and to the loa, themselves. I intuitively saw what, if the loa agreed, could be an evolution in a type of spiritual practice I love. I saw that I could be a small part of this change. I use the word "evolution" because the loa die if they are not served. To survive, the loa as well as the voodoosants must change; we must adapt to the evolving/current *Weltanschauung*. A loa who only eats human flesh and the voodoosants who serve this loa would not last long in today's New Orleans.

So do you believe that you accumulated bad karma with the blood sacrifices that you did participate in?

Yes, but then I am not sure what the Tibetans mean by karma. The closest I can come to what is meant by karma is habit. The habits one develops in this life follow and determine the quality of future lives. There are boucou schools and this may be a Middle Way School understanding of karma. I looked into the eyes of one animal before I sacrificed it and saw tremendous understanding and wisdom. I went with the ritual flow anyway and sacrificed it. During the sacrifice there was fear and pain. This is an example of what I would call not the best of habits/karma to nurture. In a dream, we are all of the characters. In this dream I did not treat a small part of myself humanly.

I distinguish between regret and guilt. I regret my actions but feel no guilt. I am sure that all I have done was necessary for me to be who I am today, this second, and I like myself a lot.

I know that Tibetan Monks are able to give up their vows and fight/kill in the name of protecting their religion, and any negative karma accumulated is considered a worthy sacrifice; in your talks with Mr Norbo was it suggested that it was your karma to perform ritual sacrifice?

No, but if a being really must be killed I would rather do it and accept the consequences than have a companion do the killing and the consequences fall to them. Maybe, in a sense, this is what love looks like. I do realize that it is very easy for me to kill, to take life. This may be the result of karma/past habits that I choose not to nurture.

Working with the orisha Obatala, who hates palm oil, must be problematic. What do you do in this situation?

Ah! For all of us, BOTH visible and invisible, it is best to make peace with our past mistakes. The white king was drunk and made a mistake. One must go on. No one is perfect. He would best forgive himself for the transgression. Once that is accomplished, the hate translates into regret and palm oil loses its emotional charge. Obatala is a tremendously large spirit., his dislike for palm oil is a small part of who s/he is. I believe that the force that is Oba Tala was, to great measure, responsible for the election of Oba Ma in the USA...

In New Orleans Voodoo, Obatala and blanc dan-i walk the same road so my dealings are with blanc dan-i. That is, in a sense, fortunate. Blanc dan- i enjoys palm oil.

You've talked of your own journey of spiritual realisation and of your relationships with the spirits but as you work within a

community I was wondering about the impact these changes in your beliefs had upon your peers?

I find that I do a good deal of teaching; a lot of sessions at festivals and other events besides rituals. Intellectual honesty and authenticity require that I show my self as I am; even if "But you wrote before" can be a bit embarrassing if one believes in a strict continuity of self.

I do tend to apologize more than usual when major shifts occur in my practice and weigh upon practices I support by drumming, etc. "I'm sorry, but now I won't be involved in rites in which ______ are sacrificed.." Years ago I was told that it takes courage to be self contradictory. I believe that I understand that statement better now.

People come and people go . . . that is the nature of life. Approval flows into disapproval and then currents reverse creating a whirlpool in which approval and its "dis" ing merge and balance. People I have worked with left. They could not be replaced but their positions and roles were taken up by others. Community shifts and one reason for the shifting can be any members change in belief.

As a bottom line, I think that selective perception is a big factor. People tend to hear what they want to hear. My beliefs may change but that change may be in large measure discounted as some sort of momentary aberration by portions of the Voodoo community.

The spilling of blood within a group context, for whatever reason, definitely creates an 'excitement' and heightened energy. How did other practitioners regard your new viewpoint and

especially in the initial stages of having non blood centred rituals, how was the participatory feel of the rites?

It's odd but the primary sentiment was one of relief. There was a realization that one does not *have* to spill blood in order to celebrate a successful rite. There is a great power in blood but needed portions of that power can be accessed by less drastic and dramatic means. Atomics are not always necessary especially if the goal of the rite is more modest than worldwide change.

Possessions, both full and partial, provide a lot of energy and excitement during the rites. Also, possessions carry within themselves the possibility of a direct involvement for large portions of the voodoosants present.. The loa or possessing spirit often seeks contact with other ritualists and gives messages and advice.

Many thanks for this Louis; it is interesting to chart the changes in your spirituality, and hear the reasons behind these changes. I would imagine working within a group practice with its established structures and traditions can tend to make re-evaluations in approach more complex.

My own evolution in practice (specifically related to blood work) as a solo practitioner had similar challenges within a different context. A main part in my own path was establishing what was right and true for myself and those that I work with, and deciding whether blood ritual was necessary as part of my own process of challenging taboos.

Interview with Ode bi tola

Ode bi tola is a Qabalistic Adept with 28 years experience and is a priest in the Cuban religion of Lukumi.

As this interview contains many terms specific to the Yoruba tradition, Ode bi tola kindly wrote this explanation of terms to help the reader.

'An orisha is a spiritual being that represents a particular aspect of God (who is called Oludumare in the Yoruba language). Oludumare created the orisha mostly to help humanity. There are however orisha of negativity such as death and misfortune.

The orisha are frequently associated with certain natural features such as thunderstorms, whirlwinds, the earth, rivers, volcanoes, rivers, swamps etc. Hence if one wishes to work with them it is better to actually visit these places as the locations act as natural temples.

Orisha are also frequently associated with the specific activities such as smithing and metalworking, hunting, divination, herbalism etc.

Orisha also are said to govern parts of the body and its

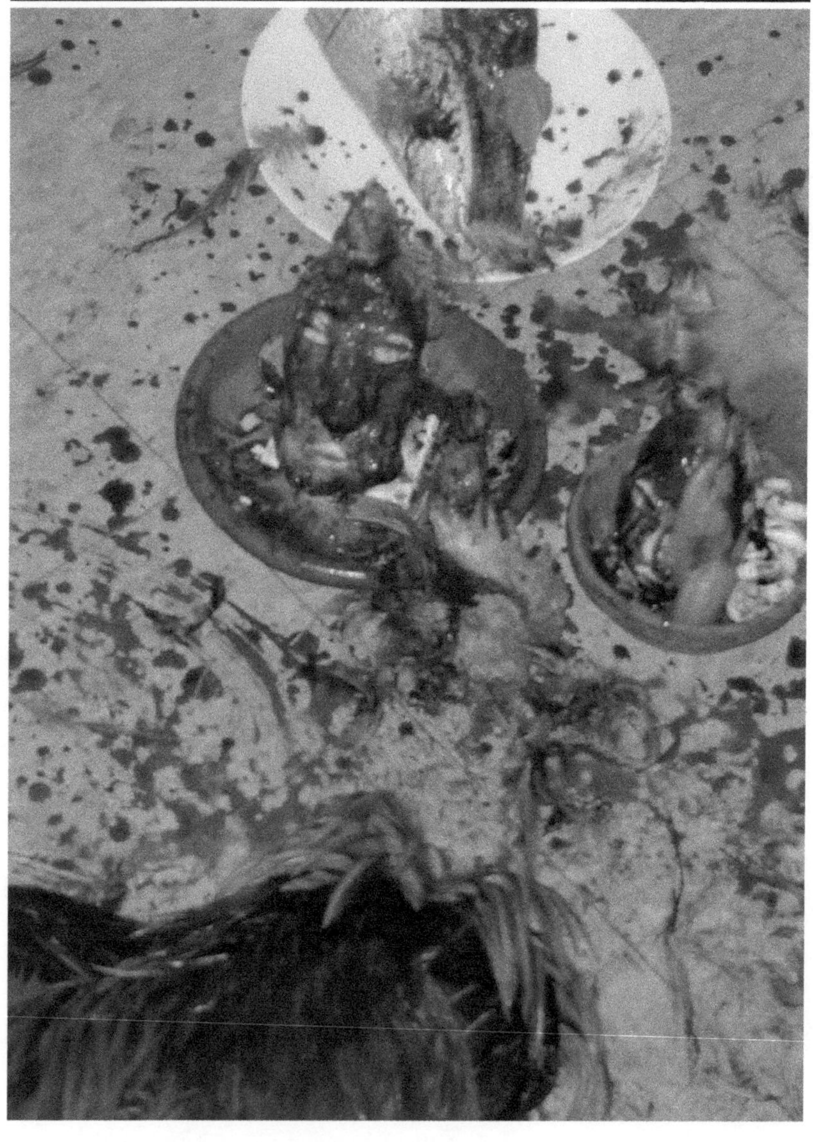

'Yoruba Sacrificial Offering'. Image by Eric K Lerner

functions. Sometimes there are overlaps between the classes of attribute each orisha has, such as Ogun who is an orisha of blacksmiths, but is also a hunting and the forest deity.

Every human being has an orisha that "walks" or resonates with them. This orisha is said to be their tutelary orisha and is seated in their head when they undergo the priest's initiation called Kariocha. Humans can communicate with the orisha via divination. The tutelary orisha is confirmed by a particular divination that is performed by a trained and very experienced orisha priest. The most accurate form of divination is done via Babalawo's who are initiated priests of the orisha of divination called Orumila.

In addition to a tutelary orisha we all have another orisha called Ori who is held to be our destiny. This orisha is said to have a function that is closer to that of the Holy Guardian Angel. Ori is deemed to be the only orisha that never leaves us. In addition, each orisha is said to have an Ori; the implication being that they must all placate their Ori at times; and also that orisha can evolve in a manner that Archangels are said not to.

As with all orisha related items there are divinatory verses from Ifa that describe Ori as the mightiest orisha. The Ifa verses are found in Eyiogbe.'

What are your thoughts on New Orleans Voodoo practitioner Louis Martinie, who amalgamated his Buddhist beliefs and his Voodoo work and uses palm oil rather than blood as an offering in rituals?

I don't know much about modern voodoo practice in New Orleans despite my godfather having had a Botanico (Magical shop) there. Voodoo in the West has two strongholds Ayti (Haiti) and New Orleans. What many people do not understand is that the voodoo deities can be traced back to Dahomey and the Fon deities in particular. Yet in Ayti there are numerous Kongo temples where the deities originated in the Kongo. The Kongo-derived religion of Palo Mayombe has a stronghold in Cuba but the Kongo religion was also heavily influential in the black communities of the American South. In fact it is argued that the firmas (ground drawing) and setting off fula (gunpowder) were Kongo contributions to the mix that is Ayti's voodoo.

'Santeria' is a word that has fallen out of vogue. The Yoruba derived religion in Cuba is now more likely to be called Lukumi as there has been a general movement to strip out the Xtian iconography that was a necessary camouflage in the old days.

A few people have voiced such opinions in Lukumi (what you call Santeria) but have often been vilified for their pains. Blood for us is the ultimate sacrifice ergo there are a host of lesser things that are sacrificed before the orisha is asked about eje (blood). There is a saying that some of the "Lagba lagba" (Lukumi for "Elder's Elders") in Cuba can achieve more with a glass of water than many of us do with a whole barnyard of chickens. It depends on what the orisha want.

I am loath to decry Mr Martinie as I have not met him. I do wonder what happens when he has a reading as are there not instances where his orisha ask for blood sacrifice? Is he initiated to the Olorisha level? As a Babalawo I know that each odu (divinatory verse) has its own prescribed blood sacrifice which is specified, as the ultimate solution to the issue as manifest by the odu. In going through the necessary corrective deeds as options to be eliminated the blood sacrifice may be the option that is required, so how one earth does he close his divinations? The orisha are living entities so they will remember what is owed to them and may raise it in the next divination or future divination.

All Lukumi and Paleros (practitioners of Palo Mayombe) have elders both living and dead so I must ask what do Mr Martinie's elders make of his anti blood stance? I assume that he does have voodoo elders but this would not be countenanced in Palo or Lukumi. However I can see it is that ultimately up to him to practice as he sees fit.

We (Paleros and Lukumi Practitioners) have very strong protocols in our work, so for anyone to come and then break away says a lot, but this is not Voodoo. I find Voodoo and Buddhism to be almost incompatible. For me both have their own beauty. The Dalai Lama is the closest to a living saint this planet has.

I know of several people that would love to get involved in the Lukumi religion but cannot pass the rubicon of blood sacrifice so they keep out.

I see no reason for an African religion to fit with European sensibilities. The mere fact that we prefer the use of the word Lukumi as opposed to Santeria reflects our desire to keep close to the roots of the southern Nigerian practice. I for one love to hurl the insult of 'new age wanker' to anyone who says otherwise. We tend to cook and eat the meat as part of a meal, unless of course it is used in a ritual cleansing. Again if there is a need for a cleansing we start off with simple baths and then move upwards to live animals.

Is scarification, piercing or tattooing utilised in a sacred context within your tradition? If so, is it the marking or the bloodletting that is effective, or both?

Scarification has no direct relevance to the Lukumi or the Paleros. Cutting is often an important question in the Lukumi and Palo experience but where there is cutting there is also an insertion of medicine below the skin. This acts as a permanent talisman. The blood that flows is often a secondary effect. At one time the Olorisha received certain head cuts but this practice seems to be in decline in certain houses in the USA. I have participated in some initiations where the head was not cut. The cut is very small and leaves a tiny scar. However cutting in Palo and certain orisha initiations to the Babalawo's court of orisha's such as Osain still occurs.

I realise Santeria, being syncretic, is a living tradition and therefore one that changes with the dictates of time. Although the US Supreme Court protects the right of Yoruba practitioners

to use animal sacrifices, what would happen if this changed? Would the orisha accept different offerings that were still appropriate? Would the lack of animal sacrifice deplete the strength of the Orisha?

Well this is an extremely controversial aspect of the religion as since Hialeah v CLB, the Oriate that successfully defended our rights notes that the practice of animal sacrifice is under siege. There is constitutional protection Lukumi practitioners are still being harassed, fined and arrested due to breaking other laws that have been specifically used against them. Such things like city zoning, humane treatment of animals and littering laws etc have resulted in allegations made against the orisha-worshipping community in the USA. In the unlikely event of the courts making animal sacrifice illegal in the USA then the community will either go underground or go to the slaughterhouses or farms to perform the necessary sacrifice. However the orisha do understand the situation that we live in and this is not a cult.

Something to bear in mind is that the practitioners of the Afro Cuban religions are intensely proud of their ability to maintain their African and or Cuban culture. American ethnic minorities are intensely proud of their birthrights and believe me everyone is an ethnic minority in America. Ha-ha. So the legal changes though unlikely will be vigorously contested.

In fact my godparent when I became a babalawo received a punitive fine for dumping animal remains in the river. This happened many months after my initiation I hasten to add. Having given the sacrifice, as per our protocols he asked where to leave the remains and was told by the orisha that they had to go to the river which he duly did but was seen by a busy-body who reported him. The orisha understand that some things need a bit of time and are willing to wait until circumstances allow such sacrifices to be performed.

What governs all of our work is the divinatory experience and the sacred verses. The Ifa corpus incessantly speaks of the need to sacrifice to return to the correct state of alignment with the individual's destiny. Sacrifice, I repeat, may be something a lot less controversial that the killing an animal. In some cases it means that we need to obtain an animal and care for it as a sacred pet. Also within the sacred odu corpus there are specific verses that discuss why human sacrifice is wrong . . . so the blood of humans is a different situation. A Nigerian friend of mine could not understand how anyone could murder another human being in peace time as the spirit of the dead man could haunt him for the rest of his life and beyond. Blood from animals is viewed in a different way but is a last resort.

Left hand path Tantra has asserted that it take one hundred drops of blood to make one drop of sperm. However, the morality of Palo and Lukumi does not allow for sexual magic so blood is the best we have. Yes in some ways the orisha may have some duress but I really don't know.

Narayan Ramos says, 'The path of blood heals you. The path of blood sacrifice heals you' Do you think that the Judaeo-Christian created taboos around blood sacrifice have created a loss within contemporary spiritual traditions?

Well the Jews still maintain the healing ritual of *Qorbanot* (how funny that they are not hassled for this practice), [Qorbanot, the Jewish term for sacrifice was once considered to be a major part of their religious ritual, and included blood sacrifice]. My daughter has had several interesting observations about the effects of this healing ritual as she is of Jewish decent.

I believe that there is a loss because the science of the larvae and dark spirits has been lost. This is something that I cannot get too far into due to my oaths but work it out for yourself.

On the plus side the orisha seem to work on the principle of 'the bigger the headache the bigger the pill'. Hence the blood sacrifice is the strongest medicine for the soul. Basically in the divination what is ascertained is the individual's path according to the destiny they received in heaven prior to incarnation. As we forget our destiny upon incarnation we blunder about and may deviate strongly from our destiny which in turn may require the sacrifice to reboot the system and maintain wellbeing. Now this rebooting can require a lot of energy for the reboot hence blood sacrifice is necessary. Also in the course of our lives we may get an attachment of a particular dark spirit which would be the linguistic equivalent of a larva in the older magical texts. These spirits are way below the hierarchy of demons but are myriad and can lead to a certain lack of well being and again it is necessary to use a bird to cleanse the individual so as to help them realise their destiny. These entities may attach themselves to even an experienced magician and may go undetected for years.

Xtianity basically works on the principles of Bhakti yoga and does not recognise the notion of personal destiny in the way that the orisha worshippers have elevated it to a personal orisha called Ori. In fact Ori is held to be the most powerful orisha as we are taught in the first of 256 odu called Baba Eyiogbe. There are verses that describe how Ori "threw" or caused the orisha to be seated in there cult centres. The narrative verse therefore describes the complete power of Ori over the orisha, in theory at least. Sometime Ori needs to be fed. The Ori is seated in the head of the individual and is fed by a ceremony requiring the head to be fed with a variety of foodstuffs which may include live chickens and or a fish.

Lukumi expect blood sacrifice to be performed by a trained individual. It is frowned upon for a non-trained initiate to do such an act. The death is very quick and humane and is similar to halal killing. The largest animal killed is a small bull which is a very rare event.

I hope that this helps

The Spaces Inbetween Interview with Eric K Lerner

ERIC K. LERNER is a priest of Obatala-Ajaguna and an accomplished writer and artist. As a writer, he has three books to his credit: *AIDS Crisis in America* (ABC-Clio, 1999); *Babalu Ayé: Santeria and the Lord of Pestilence* (Original Publications, 2000) *and Olokun, A Book of Mystery* (T& D Publications), 2003. He has also published articles on metaphysics, African-Caribbean religions and the occult in a variety of magazines, including *Shaman's Drum*, *Ashé*, *New Aeon* and *Oya N'Soro*. He has also worked as an arts reviewer and investigative reporter.

How would you define blood within the context of Santeria?

Blood, *eje*, is the most powerful offering made in Santeria. It is the ultimate means of exchange between man and God. We have a saying that without blood in the veins there cannot be life. It has been noted in many studies of African religions that blood sacrifice redistributes life force. The life force of the sacrificial animal is used to enhance the life value of the person for whom it is sacrificed. It also imparts that essence on the orisha to whom the offering is made so that the orisha will have the strength to see that the supplicant's wishes are granted.

On a personal level, I find it excruciating, exhilarating and necessary. In witnessing or implementing a sacrifice I am always viscerally reminded of the fragile nature of mortal existence and how easily it can be taken away. For me, it is difficult to perform the killing of an animal because I have empathic tendencies. I long ago noticed that I could assuage pain for someone else by placing hands on him. When killing an animal, I experience pain from its death throes. However, there are transcendent moments of stillness and peace I feel once the trauma is over. It can be likened to an orgasm, but I think that really trivializes the weight or value of what is being offered and lost. Frankly, it is not too uncommon to experience orgasm a couple of times a day. Hopefully, bridging life death boundaries is not nearly as common.

I wish to make a couple of notes about how the killing is done. (I will not fully describe how a sacrifice is performed simply because I don't want the uninitiated trying this at home.) By law, an animal sacrifice can only be mandated by direct communication from an orisha (such as through an oracle or direct verbal communication through a trance medium), and only performed by a priest who has undergone rigorous training. All present must tug the skin on his own throat when an animal is killed to remind him of the great offering the animal is making. (Usually the priest performing the sacrifice will have an assistant tug on his own throat.) Afterward, the person for whom the offering was made must reverentially raise the head of the animal from the floor to indicate his thanks to and support of the animal in its flight to heaven. I'm appalled when I hear of people embarking on an animal sacrifice without such rigorous criteria in place.

From my own experience I have discovered that most people are perfectly willing to throw their moral prohibitions about animal sacrifice out the window just to get what they want. I cannot tell you how many times I have had people come to me who had PETA (People's Ethical Treatment of Animals) bumperstickers on their cars and ask me to kill five birds for them just so they can get laid.

Does Santeria view blood from humans and blood from animals in different ways?

Yes. There is a mythic basis for why animals are used instead of humans as sacrifices in Santeria. Many years ago in a Yoruba village there was a distinguished elder named Akuko. Akuko is the Yoruba word for rooster, and rooster is the most commonly sacrificed bird in Santeria rituals. During Akuko's life an edict was issued in his village that anyone who started a fire in a sacred grove must be executed. One day Akuko walked by the grove, and saw that two children had started a fire. Not wishing the children to be punished, he took blame for the fire himself. He figured the integrity of his character would cause the edict for mandatory execution to be removed. In short, it was not.

On his way to being killed he requested that he be allowed to step into the river to wash his face. Once he did that his execution proceeded. Because killing him represented an injustice, it is believed that orisha forbade killing of humans in their honour. In deference to his gesture of washing himself, the feet and faces of birds are washed with water prior to sacrifice. Implicit in this rationale is the belief that a sacrificial animal takes the place of a person. The person on whose behalf the sacrifice is made is asked to speak to the animal prior to sacrifice to carry his wishes to heaven. Certain types of animals are felt to have blood closer to human than others, and that may determine circumstances under which those animals are used.

The types of animals used in sacrifices are unique to the orisha being honoured. For instance, the orisha Eleggua is given roosters and pigeon blood is taboo for him. Pigeon blood cannot touch any representation of him. The colour and gender of the animals also is specific to each individual orisha. Ultimately that (and other types of offerings given to orisha) is based on a system of sympathies and antipathies familiar to occult practitioners from the works of Agrippa. The use of human blood is forbidden.

Do priests ever use their own blood in rites?
No.

If a priest has an injury or cut is there a different criterion as to how he works or how he performs rituals?
For me, certainly there is. I try to avoid participating in blood rites if I have an open sore or injury. That could be an abscess tooth or a hernia. Simply, I do not want the orisha to mistake my own blood for the blood being offered and to develop a taste for it. I believe most other priests I know share that belief. However, I still will take part in ritual activities during times of injury, and try to avoid those aspects of ritual which involve life force offering. Let me provide a simple instance. Last year, I was asked to assist in giving the deity Olokun. I had just aggravated a hernia through some ill-timed heavy lifting. When it came time to perform the Mantanzas (the blood offering to empower the birth of the orisha) I was selected to take

the recipient to the ocean in order to guide him through another aspect of the initiation. When I returned with him, the blood sacrifices had been completed and I continued to assist in the remaining steps of the ceremony.

Is menstrual blood used in any rites?

No. There is a taboo about menstruating women taking part in rituals. The taboo has a mythic basis. There was a time when the orisha Yemaya desired to learn the secrets of cowrie shell divination from her husband Orunla. Orunla wished to discover who was trying to learn his secrets, and discovered that it was Yemaya because she left a trail of her menstrual blood behind her. Since it was her menstrual blood that betrayed Yemaya, Olofi, God, instructed her to use the time of her menses to honour God, rest and meditate on the mysteries of life and faith that she wished to master. Since then women have followed her example, and do not work with religious mysteries during their periods. It is said that they should use that time to meditate, honour divinity, and allow their bodies to rest. As a sidebar it is interesting to note, that story is also used to explain why Yemaya is regarded as a special protector of gay men, since it is gay men who give her safe harbour to escape her husband's rage. So the story itself seems to be used to explain different taboo behaviours.

Is blood of any sort used in any medicines, fetish objects or charms?

Certainly animal blood is an integral part of many medicinal, fetish and reliquary preparations. The incarnations of orisha are nourished with sacrificial blood. (The orisha are incarnated in stones and shells that are generally kept in pots.) There is no life without blood in the veins and an orisha does not continue to exist in the stones without blood nourishment. Interestingly, the orisha are brought into being through incantations and immersion in herbal infusions. The blood offering is made afterward. For me, I feel that the blood acts as a kind of wake up call, the introduction of animating force.

Reading up on ritual use of blood in other traditions I came across various mentions of the fact that if an animal sacrifice is used, it is only a domestic animal; is the same in Santeria?
The most common types of animals used in Santeria sacrifices are goats, rams, turtles, aguties (a type of large rodent), roosters, hens, guinea hens, ducks, doves, and pigeons. The types of animals used are specific to the orisha being honoured. If you can catch a pigeon or turtle in the wild, that's fine. Some priests raise the animals they sacrifice.

Are there any guidelines as to age, general health, or gender of the animal used?
Yes. Every orisha has very specific guidelines as to what types of animal they accept. Each has taboo animals. The purpose of this is to employ sympathetic energy forces that reverberate with the orisha. Using an unhealthy animal is viewed unfavourably, since it would provide the orisha with attenuated life force.

In your article "Babalu" you used a quote from Narayan Ramos, "The path of blood heals you. The path of blood sacrifice heals you." Do you think that the Judaeo-Christian created taboos around blood sacrifice have created a loss within contemporary spiritual traditions?

Yes. I think there is a loss of spiritual immediacy in most religions of the book. To me, they seem to borrow piece-meal from older traditions and beliefs that once played a lot more active roles in people's life. Santeria does not create a dichotomy between one's spiritual and earthly nature the way religions of the book do. Attainment of happiness is based on what we experience here and now, and not something we put off until after death. Heaven and earth mirror one another. God and the orisha animate every conscious and subconscious action. That being said, I believe that each individual has free will to make responsible decisions about what type of spirituality works best for him, and it is not up to me as a Santeria priest to make that decision for him. Whenever a Santeria ritual of any kind is performed, the priest must say to his client, "We join with the orisha," and the client must respond, "I join with the orisha of my free will," before the ritual can proceed. One of the first lessons I received in Santeria is that a Santeria priest must never proselytize. The orisha are fully capable of letting someone know if they want him to interact with them. Therefore, I fully believe that everyone can decide and realize what type of religion works for him. I hope that it is a conscious decision, and not something tantamount to following the crowd.

Although the US Supreme Court presently protects the right of Yoruba Santeria followers to use animal sacrifices what would happen if this changed?

We've kept our rituals more or less intact for something like five thousand years. We practiced animal sacrifice underground when it was illegal here, and if necessary we will do so again.

Would the Orisha accept different offerings that were still appropriate?

No. Not when it is mandated. However, the orisha do accept other forms of offering, including: herbal infusions, foods, objects of beauty, commitments of work, and prayer. There is room for negotiation, which is why a priest who is knowledgeable in communicating with orisha should mediate offerings. There are times when a blood sacrifice is employed when another offering could achieve the same ends. Remember, that a blood sacrifice is the most powerful and tantalizing offering for an orisha. Put yourself in the orisha's situation. If you were hungry and someone gave you a choice between a gourmet meal and a fast food takeout you would probably choose the gourmet meal. However, if you were just offered the fast food, you would likely accept it. It is a similar situation with orisha.

A priest must know how to negotiate. For instance, if I wish for the holy mother of the world, Yemaya to assist me with a financial boon I could ask her through an oracle if she would do so in return for an offering of fried pork rinds and plantains. In my experience in dealing with her most gracious and kind nature, she might well say yes. If instead, I offered her a rooster immediately, could you blame her if she said yes to that? I believe a priest has a responsibility to suggest other potentially suitable offerings to the orisha first. Other priests have different opinions on that matter.

In the real world frying pork rinds generates a thick veil of black smoke, and there is a risk of grease splatter, not to mention that you have to leave it by Yemaya for seven days and then take it to a body of water. Dispatching a rooster takes a few minutes, and for some priests is an easier task. Because where I live, birds require some effort to obtain and I experience physical pain in making a life force offering, I am more inclined to suggest other offerings first. People have free will and must live with the consequences they invite. I realize that not every priest shares my situation, so I will not judge anyone too harshly for choosing to offer a blood offering first. The fact is that it will almost always be accepted, and requires less thought than figuring out what other offerings might also be suitable.

Would the lack of animal sacrifice deplete the strength of the Orisha?

An orisha cannot be born or called into existence without blood sacrifice. When you enter into the priesthood, you agree to keep your orisha happy. A lot of the time, I give them artwork in which I invest a lot of effort rather than blood, and often they express satisfaction with me for that. But if they insist on blood because of their own needs, I exist for them as much as they exist for me, and I personally do not stomach well people who make half baked commitments of any kind.

When you say that you exist for the orisha as much as they exist for you, you seem to indicate a symbiotic relationship of sorts between you?

Certainly it is a reciprocal relationship. The orisha exist for us as much as we exist for them. We put a name on them and differentiate them from other forms of energy. Also, orisha, like most African deities, have mostly evolved from ancestors. One story of how orisha came to be worshipped goes like this. Originally when men began to die, it was believed that their spirits would enter heaven. When it rained their spirits rose into the sky and returned to earth in rain. The spirits found homes in river stones. People began to gather these stones in pots to revere their ancestors and ask their guidance and intervention in worldly endeavours. Eventually, people realized that certain families possessed stones that were more efficacious than others in granting petitions. These especially effective ancestor spirits came to be venerated by larger and larger communities, and thus orisha were born.

In a sense, orisha priests seek to so identify with their orisha that they become part of how their orisha is perceived. You can find an antecedent for this in the *Egyptian Book of the Dead* where you read the descendant's name being referred to as "Osiris Ani." The priest becomes part of the larger godhead. Part of how we come to know an orisha is through their children, priests who are their mortal incarnations and representatives. I gave you the example of someone who has Shango as a tutelary deity is likely to be charismatic, dynamic and promiscuous, and that these qualities are akin with Shango. This statement is based on direct observation of people who have Shango as a tutelary deity.

When we pray in Santeria, we begin our prayer with praise statements to God Almighty and then name deceased priests in our spiritual lineages and blood ancestors before we name orisha. There is a famous Yoruba saying that there are no orisha without ancestors. Human beings represent vital clues to how we understand deity. In a sense, I aspire to become part of how people understand my own deity, Obatala Ajaguna.

Do the orisha make sacrifice of themselves, or make sacrifice themselves?

The stories which chronicle the mortal lives of orisha are mostly tragic in nature. Tragedy is a means by which a human actor is transformed into a transcendent figure that is a means to the godhead for those who come after him. Sacrifice means to make sacred. So in their mortal spans the Orisha did make themselves sacred by giving of themselves. In their roles as administrators of god force, I do not necessarily see them as making sacrifices of themselves. They employ or redirect life energy to satisfy the needs of the supplicant.

Regarding areas in which blood is spilled in a deliberate but non ritualised manner (battle zones, areas where a murder is committed, hospitals); does your tradition view these areas as contaminated, dangerous or having any particular energy about them?

Like many spiritual traditions, we are sensitive to spiritual energies. I feel that a place maintains signatures of events that have occurred there. These can be positive as well as negative. I still get a special feeling when I walk down the New York City street where I first met my late life partner. In terms specific to Santeria, places of violence, such as hospitals, are taboo to priests during their novitiate year because they may be especially sensitive to the discordant energies unleashed in such places. I have noticed that I myself feel most at peace in Switzerland because there has been little recent history of war or a high violent crime rate there. In going into a city such as Baltimore, which has one of the highest violent crime rates in the world, I get physically sick.

What are your thoughts on the New Orleans Voodoo Temple practitioner and priest Louis Martinie who amalgamated his Buddhist beliefs and his Voodoo work and uses palm oil rather than blood in rituals?

If that works for Martinie, I wish him well. Blood and palm oil are very different. Palm oil is a human food. In Yoruba culture, a child is anointed with palm oil during baptism so that he will be able to recognize food and not go hungry in his life. It is not equivalent to a life force offering. Palm oil is pleasing to many orisha as a food or unguent. It does not make things happen like blood does. A life force offering calls things into being and acts as first cause. A food offering disposes the orisha well toward the person who offers it, but that is not the same as making something happen. Also, think about it, if you were undergoing surgery would you be happy or secure to hear that the surgical team had ordered a couple pints of Palm oil rather than the appropriate blood type for you?

Are scarification, piercing, or tattooing utilised in sacred context within your tradition? If so is it the marking, the bloodletting or a combination of both which creates the effect?

No. It is taboo for a Santeria priest to undergo any type of piercing, tattooing or scarification because his body houses an orisha. A priest's body is a temple of ocha. For me, this proved very empowering. When I was first diagnosed with HIV, it was considered a death sentence. That raised a lot of issues for me regarding physical intimacy. How can you share your body with somebody in a love act when you know that you may in effect be killing him or her by transmitting a fatal virus? It caused me to feel that I was a biohazard. Plus, it was not uncommon to find myself in social situations where people would refuse to shake my hand. One point of Santeria etiquette is to make *moforibale* that is to prostrate yourself at the feet of a senior priest to ask his blessing and for him to raise you (Theologically, it is believed that priest's orisha does the raising.) Once I became a priest, people were prostrating themselves at my feet and asking me to raise them. Can you imagine what that felt like in light of the experiences I had as a socially stigmatized person? I began to think of myself very differently. Today, I honestly believe that if I allow people to get close to me physically I'm extending a privilege to them. I view my physical being as one honoured to represent a living deity.

Your mention of the priest's body being a home for the ocha and needing to be treated accordingly is interesting. A proportion of people that I have talked to involved with ritualised scarification and body mortification are also spiritually affiliated to Northern Traditions where the god form they house or link with such as Loki or Odin, went through mortifications similar to the ones they choose to undergo.

To pick up on another point in your answer to the last question, I did talk to one Lukumi Priest who said that in the Palo Tradition there was a ritualised cutting in which a 'medicine is inserted under the skin', and any blood flow is merely a secondary effect. However he made no mention of whether this ritual was given by a priest or given to a priest.

I checked on this. Often there is a powder applied to the wounds after the incision is made. This effectively seals off the wound and aids in recognizable scarring (cuts in Palo are made in particular places and the resulting scars aid paleros in recognizing one another.) To me this does not negate the power of the blood flow. However, I am *regardo** (the marks on me were made with chalk and not a razor since I had already made ocha at the time I was initiated). I may not be the best qualified person to talk about this, and would prefer to concentrate on Ocha in which my experience is more typical.

I don't know if you ever came across the 1980s book *Modern Primitives* that looked at body piercing/tattooing and body modification as a way of expressing individuality and also of connecting with an atavistic spirituality? I consider the above acts to be blood rites that are essentially spiritual in nature, though this spiritual act may be an unconscious one. In context of our discussion thus far, do you have any opinion on this?
Ultimately, I believe that transgressive visual and performance art must be subjected to the same criteria as other art. It is very easy if you are intellectually savvy and hip to conceive some titillating act that people would be willing to pay money to witness. You can charge a fair amount of money to perform a kitchen table castration at an "alternative" art gallery, and I've know people who have done so. Whether that qualifies, as art is another question.

I believe that in regard to body modification as art the individual

---

* In Palo the basic initiation requires the initiate to receive incisions, and is called *rayamiento*. However if that initiate has already become a santeria priest it is forbidden that his skin be broken or modified. Hence he receives chalk marks where the incisions are normally made which is them termed a *regardo* rather than a *rayamiento*.

artist should ask himself first whether the same or even more powerful effect could be achieved through creating a work of literary or visual artistic impression, or if indeed the act will express a higher artistic value through public performance. Not every work of art is going to please everyone and fit everyone's cultural values. As an artist, I believe you have an obligation to be honest with what you seek to express and define your own boundaries. I myself used to work as a performance artist and was versed in Artaud's theory of Theatre of Cruelty. It did inform some of the work I did (although I believe my fundamental sensibility leaned more toward Epic Theatre) Because of my religious beliefs, I cannot even consider doing anything that involves my own body modification now. I also could not perform some of the pieces I once did. However, I believe that you can present ideas of substance through such public performances, but you don't merit a free pass for just being blatant about anything.

In a practical sense, does your being HIV positive make a difference to the way you work within your tradition?
No. However, my experience with HIV motivates me to be more inclined to spiritually minister to those who face serious illness, trauma, or social stigmas.

Does it change your status within the tradition?
No. In general I have been treated with the same respect any other priest is. I did have a godchild leave because he said he could not understand how a priest could face the type of life challenges that I did. However, he was not from a background that embraced Santeria, and I think he became involved with the religion to satisfy his own self image as a hipster who embraced an outside culture.

I have heard accounts of HIV positive people who experienced prejudice from Santeria practitioners. One example occurred in which a number of priests refused to perform a priesthood initiation for an AIDS patient. They used the argument that you cannot give ocha to the dead. However at the time, there was a great deal of prejudice toward HIV positive people in society as a whole. Santeros are human and make human mistakes. I don't feel the prejudice those priests exhibited was (or is) unique to them as Santeros. When I was initiated, my padrino asked me to provide him with some Spanish language literature about HIV transmission so that he could share it with the priests who assisted in the ritual. Maybe education made a difference there, and people given the facts made reasonably enlightened decisions about whether or not to participate in my initiation. None of them displayed any prejudiced behaviour toward me, and the initiation followed the same series of rituals that any other such initiation would.

Is this perspective the same in America as in other countries practising Santeria, or is it a necessary modernisation?

I don't know.

Do Western belief systems which you encountered have a similar figure to Babalu with the ability to empower their devotees through affliction from disease.

Obviously St. Lazarus. Although St. Lazarus or San Lazaro is one of the most beloved saints universally, he was not an historic figure. Rather he is the beggar referred to in a memorable parable related in Luke, xvi, 19-31:

"There was a certain rich man, which was clothed in purple and fine linen, and fared sumptuously every day:

And there was a certain beggar named Lazarus, which was laid at his gate, full of sores,

And desiring to be fed with the crumbs which fell from the rich man's table: moreover the dogs came and licked his sores.

And it came to pass, that the beggar died, and was carried by the angels into Abraham's bosom: the rich man also died, and was buried;

And in hell he lift up his eyes, being in torments, and seeth Abraham afar off, and Lazarus in his bosom.

And he cried and said, Father Abraham, have mercy on me, and send Lazarus that he may dip the tip of his finger in water, and cool my tongue; for I am tormented in this flame.

But Abraham said, Son, remember that thou in thy lifetime receivedst thy good things, and likewise Lazarus evil things: but now he is comforted, and thou art tormented.

And beside all this, between us and you there is a great gulf fixed: so that they which would pass from hence to you cannot; neither can they pass to us, that would come from thence.

Then he said, I pray thee therefore, father, that thou wouldest send him to my father's house:

For I have five brethren; that he may testify unto them, lest they also come into this place of torment.

Abraham saith unto him, they have Moses and the prophets; let them hear them.

And he said, nay, father Abraham: but if one went unto them from the dead, they will repent.

And he said unto him, if they hear not Moses and the

> prophets, neither will they be persuaded, though one rose from the dead."

The passage contains many of the elements associated with Lazaro: poverty, skin afflictions, the colour purple (that ironically is taken from the rich man to be attributed to Lazaro's iconography), dogs, and an absence of water, the virtue of humility and the promise of resurrection. These are all attributions of Babaluaye. There is often confusion over Lazarus' Christian identity due to Christ's resurrection of his friend Lazarus and the existence of a Bishop of Milan by the same name.

However, it is the beggar who has endured and continues to inspire. Lazaro has been associated with aiding the sick and poor since the Middle Ages. It was during that time that word "Lazaretto' was coined to mean hospital and "Lazrone" to mean beggar.

In 1090 the Order of St. Lazarus of Jerusalem was founded. This was a chivalric order that cared for lepers and the afflicted in general. Members of the order were called Lazarists or Lazarites. They took over a leprosarium outside of Jerusalem that had been founded by St. Basil in the 4th Century of the Common Era. By the time that the Christian were expelled from the Holy Land in the 13th Century, the Order moved its headquarters to France. They proceeded to establish leprosarium's, knows and "lar-cottes" or "lazarettes" through virtually all of Europe and Britain. Since that time, Lazaro has gained cultus as the special patron for those disenfranchised by both illness and poverty. Today, many AIDS hospices in Europe bear his name.

Interestingly, accordingly to legend, the original defenders of the Order of St. Lazarus were themselves lepers. The image of Leper-Warrior melds with that of the awesome orisha Babaluaye, depicted in Africa as a formidable leprosy or smallpox-afflicted warrior king. Lazaro's identification with Babaluaye in both Cuba and Brazil began when the first Yoruba and Fon slaves arrived in the New World two centuries ago. The identification and syncretisation between the West African demigod and Saint is probably the most complete. Many Lukumi priests who would never dream of calling Shango "Santa Barbara" refer to Babaluaye as "Lazaro," "El Viejo Lazaro," or "Lazarito." Interestingly, priests who either channel Babaluaye or are considered especially knowledgeable in his medicines are also called "Lazaritos,' similar to the way Knight of the Order were called Lazarites.

Perhaps because San Lazaro represents a universal spirit who did not have a specific antecedent has made it so easy to see him and Babaluaye as being one and the same spirit. Lazaro is also syncretised with Legba, the opener of the gate in Haitian Vodou. Lazaro is embraced by curanderos as well. Interestingly, there is little mention of any lwa corresponding to Babaluaye. However, the attributes of Legba in many ways resemble Babaluaye's. In the Cuban Arara religion that developed Fon religion, possibly the biggest contributor to the Vodou pantheon, and the highest deity in its pantheon is Asoyi – a manifestation of Babalu. Perhaps, some future researcher/devotee might examine the relationship between Babaluaye and the Haitian Legba in light of this.

Hmmm, it's intriguing that Babaluaye could be seen to have a correspondence to Legba...who is considered to be the lwa that opens the gateways. I find it especially interesting if I consider the standardised criterion of Shamanic initiation where illness and affliction are gifts that bestow the ability to cross over to other realms?

Do you believe that HIV could be viewed in the same way in which Shamanic Traditions view illnesses or near death experiences, as an initiatory rite and a necessary descent into an underworld in order to gain knowledge and power?

In a sense, yes. It has been observed by many scholars that Santeria, like other African religions, is fundamentally a religion of healing. Most priests I know were motivated to embark on a priesthood initiation because of some life trauma. As a result, there is often a sense among Santeria practitioners that a critical illness may be the orisha's way of calling someone to the religion.

On the other hand, I know of some people who made the saint because they wished professional gain or wanted to express thanks to the orisha for some personal boon. So it might be a little pretentious to say that ocha represents a healing rite for everyone. One thing my late padrino taught me was that you cannot judge anyone else's motives for entering the priesthood too closely, because the orisha are fully capable of bringing about the necessary circumstances to require such an act, and you may not ultimately be able in the here and now to know where an individual's priesthood may lead him.

For instance, someone could make the saint because he just won the lottery and comes from a family culture in which making the saint is a cool thing to do. Next year, after making the saint, he may find out that he has a terminal disease and really needs the orisha to help him deal with that physical ordeal. Maybe in light of the help he receives, he becomes a compassionate priest. He helps many people with their own challenges. Now when first seeing him, I might think "Golly gee, he's a poseur." In that case I would find myself proven wrong.

I know that one of the priests told me after my novitiate year that he had me pegged wrong. He thought that I was just an arrogant white person looking for a literary experience, but he came to believe that I was very sincere in my faith. He was an elder priest, and probably someone who thought he could judge people well. In light of that experience, I'd rather extend to people benefit of the doubt.

Pre your diagnosis with HIV was your creative process such a dominant aspect of your life?

Creative expression has always been vital to me. I think it is one of the greatest gifts my orisha Obatala who embodies creativity, has benefited me with, and I would not like to think about what my life would have been if I were not blessed with openness on all levels to embrace creative strategies.

I hope that you do not find me sensationalist and insensitive, but I'd really like you to go into this a bit more for me, as your HIV status seemed to have so much to do with your relationship with Santeria and your creative process. As you have already said, your art has always been an important part of your life but I'm interested in how this process has changed. You have

mentioned that you are unable to do self mortifications of any sort as your body houses your orisha and also that you give the orisha offerings of your art work.

This all shows, to me, a sense of the sacred about your self expression that did not exist before, or existed in a different way? You said that you went from feeling like a "walking biohazard" to having a strength and empowerment.

I'm interested in hearing more about this change and the creative processes that accompanied it?

I can only try to answer you through the lens of my own experience. I do not believe that *ocha** or any shamanistic initiation substantially changes who you are. Rather it teaches you to value who you are and recognize that you yourself are part of a greater consciousness. In the case of Santeria, the consciousness is embodied in orisha. In the kariocha initiation, you are in a sense married to your orisha. Your orisha represents both a deity and the highest expression of the type of consciousness you possess. It motivated me to assign a positive value to myself and my self expression. However, I think that I always did have a gut sense that my opinions and how I expressed them mattered.

Most artists have rather substantial egos. The kariocha initiation helped me focus and recognize that I was not completely defined by

---

* An abbreviation for kariocha, the ritual in which one receives the mysteries of one's tutelary orisha and becomes a priest.

the circumstances of my illness, economics or upbringing. After all, it is pretty rare that a white boy raised Protestant – and who rejected that religion – would become a priest in an ancient African religion. So the sense of possibility I had about myself and what I could achieve became greater. It also enabled me to understand the world around me better. I began to perceive some method to the madness. Existence and history became part of a pattern defined by comprehensible and accessible spiritual energy.

The Fon, who are neighbours of the Yoruba and who influenced Yoruba culture and theology, have a saying, "It's all happened before in Heaven so that it can happen again on earth." When you begin to understand something, you feel a measure of control. One of the important lessons anyone who survives with a life threatening disease often learns is that you have to educate yourself about your affliction. In that way you take ownership of the course of treatment on which you decide. You assume a measure of control over what is happened to you. Similarly, understanding life from a spiritual perspective also helps you feel that you can master your own ship.

Having undergone a radical spiritual journey I was more willing to make radical choices in my life because I realized that I could make such a dramatic transformation. I had always wanted to pursue the visual arts, but had no training and certainly had come to believe that such a pursuit was no longer possible. The fact that I was able to make ocha in middle age helped me believe that I could pursue my desires even if the conventions imposed by society and our educational system discouraged those pursuits.

Of course, feeling that I had and continue to have the orisha and the ancestors on my side is a big help. I sometimes joke that Obatala was looking around for a painter, and since no one of any pre established credentials was presenting himself he decided to settle on me. At least I was willing. Remember that he is a deity of laughter as much as of creativity.

That's as self-effacing as I'll get. I think also that making ocha did reinforce my work ethic. It is an expensive endeavour that also requires a lot of commitment. I believe that whatever success I achieve artistically has a lot to do with putting on the elbow grease and sticking to the process. When you have achieved anything in your life through hard work and effort you learn that other goals are achievable the same way. Anyone who has made ocha whom I know is proud of what he has done.

To get back to your original question, I believe a lot of the thoughts and emotions that I express creatively now were part of my psychological and spiritual makeup before I made ocha. Hopefully, ocha provides me with an energy channel that allows the creative expressions to flow through me in a positive manner. In a sense, we learn from our orisha that they each embody a positive and negative expression illustrated through the fables associated with them. By recognizing how one's orisha was able to realize his own divine nature, one is able to try to do so too.

In the book which you recommended to me, *Santeria Aesthetics*, artists such as Jose Bedia make a very clear delineation between their art and their religion.

However artists such as Ana Mendieta (though admittedly some of her work was political as well as religious) did not have the same boundaries. How does Santeria view religious art work which uses blood, such as that which was created by Mendieta?
In the case of Mendieta, I do not know if she had made *Santo**, and that would have bearing on doctrinal perspective on her work. In general, the taboo on a priest using his blood products, hair, nail clippings, etc. in creative work relates on a practical level to an issue of personal safety as well as taboos on body modification. If someone acquires your physical residue he is in position to work effective black magick on you. In general, allowing that type of open access to you is not considered a good thing for anyone who practices Santeria (or people in general.) Of course, for a priest that carries a special weight since a priest is regarded as an elite person whose sustained well being has ramifications for the entire community and orisha. As an artist who is also a priest I recognize a lot of the issues of responsibility raised by both. As an artist, I have always embraced a take no prisoner's attitude, and feel an essential obligation to be completely honest in my work. It is a widely recognized truth that every artist has a spousal obligation to his intimate muse, and that relationship comes first (in regard to Santeria there are doctrinal perspectives as far as what that muse may be.) My work has often been perceived as transgressive. Frankly, I think everyone has to

---

* Spanish for Saint and slang for an orisha. When used in greetings, one says "benediction", if the person receiving the salutation is a priest they will reply "Santo" which is taken to mean "may the orisha bless you."

question the values of society and examine how he relates to it. I don't respect people who lead unexamined lives.

Artists who are religious, whatever their beliefs, often feel special challenges defined by their expressed beliefs and values in religious doctrines versus their individual self expression. After all, if you are going to question society and how you relate to it, your religious community is a society with which you are well acquainted. In my estimation, I'm not giving the Santeria community a free pass on that score.

On the other hand, I realize that I have entered into a contract with the orisha as a priest and enjoy many privileges because of that. For the most part, ethically I do not feel there is much contradiction particularly since my orisha Obatala is a deity of creative expression, judgement and war. When it comes to art, I think he gets it and would not respect his son for not holding his art to a standard of truth, however difficult that may be for a lot of people to accept. Frankly, I recognize that the majority of those in the Santeria community would be a lot more receptive to my depictions of orisha if they were of a more *Hallmark* greeting card variety. The public in general likes kind of idealized safe depictions of icons of their religious beliefs. Santeros are no different. As personal litmus, I am not going to take things at a face value. I believe that part of my initiatic knowledge as a priest gives me a means to directly and honestly perceive orisha.

As an artist, I have an obligation to reveal what my own truth is. If I have a question about the veracity of my work, I have means to oracles by which the orisha speak. In those times where I might question the decisions I make, they, the orisha, have always given me the thumbs up. However, I am willing to accept it if they do not.

This is not to say that I do not ever make social concessions to being a priest. I honour taboos about body modification, public nudity, use of my own blood, etc., that I perhaps I would not were I not a priest. Certainly, I did not observe all three aforementioned taboos when I was a professional performer prior to making the saint. I also believe that it is important to make the distinction that I speak for myself as an artist when I grant a public interview as opposed to being a spokesperson for Santeria. Also, because Santeria is a religion that has been subjected to some very inaccurate and unflattering stereotypes, I am conscious about perpetuating those stereotypes through public speaking or interviews. As in any type of pattern of human interactions, I have had some negative experiences with other santeros. As a rule, I do not seek to amplify them in my public speaking because I believe there is a lot of good and sense of community in the religion that is by and large overlooked by the popular media, and I don't want things blown out of context. However, art must always speak for itself and be judged independently on its own merit. Once you give birth to a work of art that work lives on its own.

Blood on the threshold: Seth demonic initiator

Lecture delivered to the 13th Oxford Golden Dawn Occult Society Thelemic Symposium.

1. 'Before me in the East Nephthys
Behind me in the West Isis
On my right hand in the South is Set
And on my left hand in the North is Horus
For above me shines the body of Nuit
And below me extends the ground of Geb
And in the centre abideth the 'Great Hidden God.'

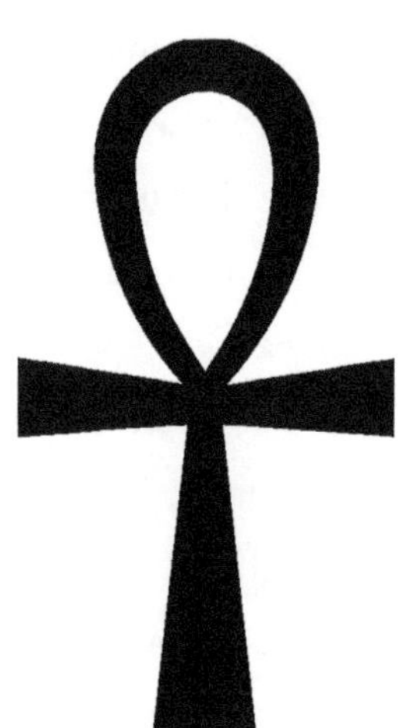

Blood

There many ways to show how important blood is in old time magical-religion. Because I am particularly drawn to the reconstructed Egyptian or Kemetic tradition I couldn't help but start with the famous, ubiquitous image of the "ankh". It's the most famous of all hieroglyphs and one of the few to survive into the Christian era where is becomes the early Christian "Chi Ro" sign.

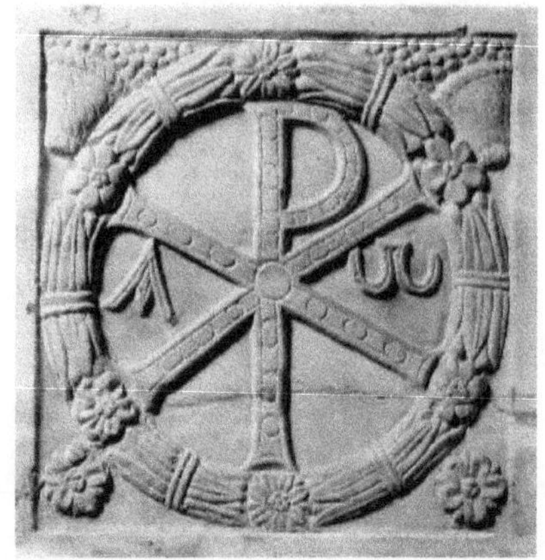

It's linguistic meaning or connotation is "Life". Egyptian hieroglyphs are pictograms representing actual objects – so what object does it represent? Some, such as Aleister Crowley thought it looked like a sandal and thus had a mystical connotation of the journey or path through life.

Recently I came across another explanation of its meaning, one that directly links it to blood. The story begins almost 100 years ago (the exact date is lost) when Margaret Murray participated in a groundbreaking public dissection of two mummies who have since been labelled "Two Brothers" and are displayed in Manchester Museum. Turns out they are two very controversial mummies. A recent controversy revolved around whether they are really two "Brothers" or two "Lovers"! Brothers, Lovers and indeed twins can generate a lot of heat in Egyptology. Greg Reeder, the current editor of popular Egyptology magazine *Kemet* and also a gay activist found himself at the centre of the "storm". The topic of "Brothers" and "Lovers" also evokes controversial issues connected with the mythology of the gods Horus & Seth, twin brothers who were also lovers!

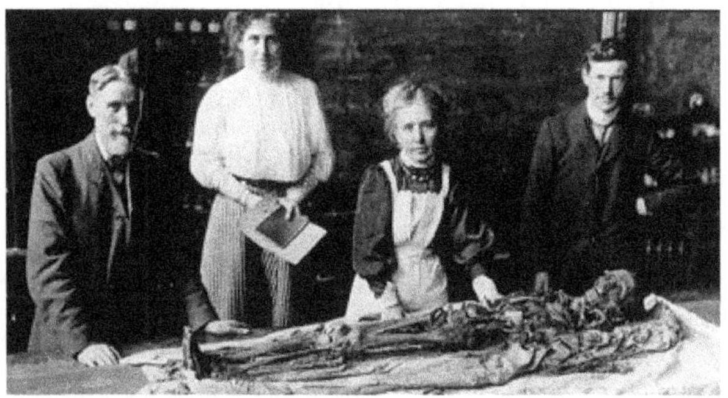

The anatomist soon discovered that one of the brothers was a eunuch and had in ancient times, undergone a remarkable operation of known as sub-incision (more of that in a moment).

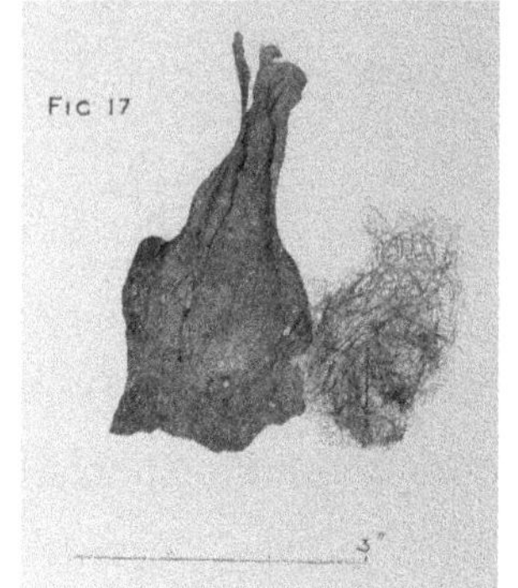

He also suggested that the wrapping of the genitals – was connected to the Egyptian "Ankh" hieroglyph and moreover it is this that gives it it's core meaning. In 1966 the German medical historian Wolfhart Westendorf said more.

He was studying a series of "knot" or "bandaging" spells in the London Medical Papyrus that were utilized to dam up bleeding from the vagina and anus, to prevent miscarriage and to thus preserve "life". The physical artefact used in conjunction with these medical spells was called "the Knot of Isis".

One way or another it is the prototype of the "ankh". The spell is to be read over a red amulet or the bound menstrual cloth or dam perhaps not too unlike a modern tampon. It reads:

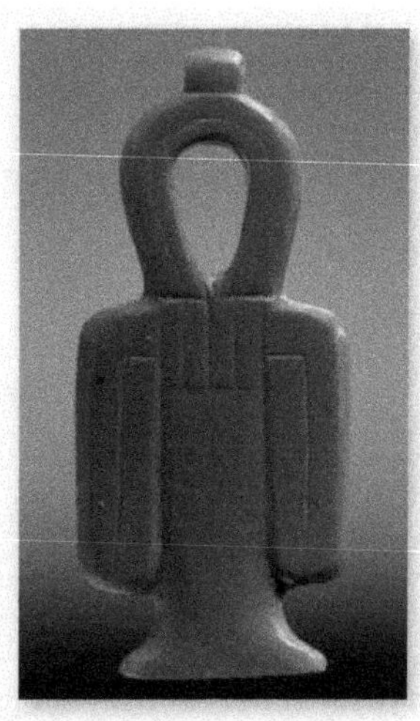

"Go back, Companion of Horus!
Go back, Companion of Seth!
From Hermopolis, Thoth has come
And he repulses the blood,

He refuses to let the red blood come now.
Pay attention to this dam
In the name of Thoth. return!

This very old spell has its origins in the Egyptian Neolithic and its cattle cults, thousands, perhaps as much as six thousand years ago. In it we see Thoth as the healer; we see Horus & Seth the two brothers, connected with blood; the menstrual cycle; and the moon. The two brothers have dangerous "companions" in the form of blood. It is this that attracts the presence of jealous ancestral spirits, who can menace the foetus in the womb.

The subject matter inevitably takes us back to a very distance past. Several very old myths survive from this time, one of the oldest known to us from Egyptian sources is "The Destruction of Humanity" the earliest version of which in told in "The Book of the Heavenly Cow" (See Erik Hornung 1999). The myth tells of human rebellion against the gods and their "all father" the sun god Ra. He retaliates, sending an emissary from his fiery solar eye, the goddess Hathor to cull the "divine cattle" i.e. human beings. (Some may know this from a Middle Kingdom version where the emissary is the leonine goddess Sekhmet).

Whether it's Hathor or Sekhmet, they both become mad with blood lust and the human cull becomes genocide. I wonder why the all powerful Ra would be concerned – after all he could just start again? Perhaps those early mythographers are aware of rebellious humanity's uniqueness.

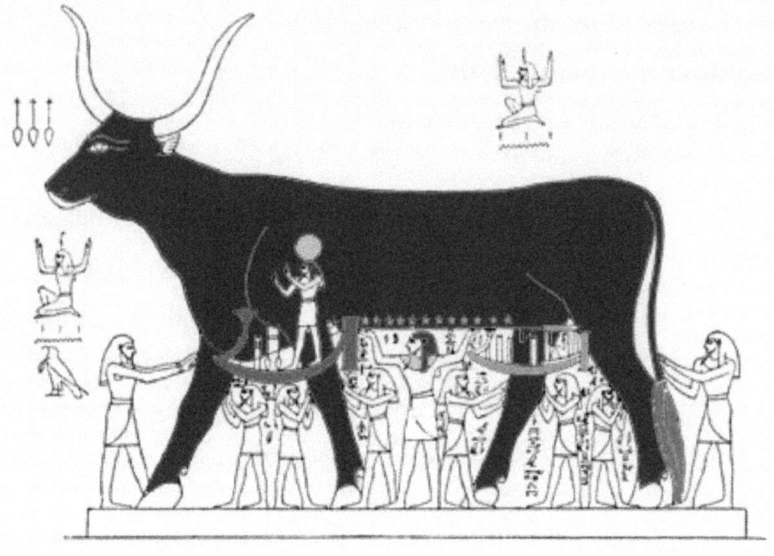

The solution to the problem of genocide is to offer Hathor her favourite tipple - more blood; and indeed from time immemorial this was the food of all gods. She is however stopped in the tracks with false blood, in fact beer laced with ochre to taste like blood. In my opinion such myths emerge at moment of crisis and change. Beer is after all an agricultural product contingent upon the grain production of the so-called Neolithic revolution of 5th millennial BC. This reminds us of the centrality of blood in sacrifice but also that there is an alternative, at least for the human variety. Henceforth save for very special times of need, the "fake" blood is all that is needed.

> "All acts of love and pleasure are my rituals" (Crowley's Liber LXV, "The Law of Liberty.")

Hathor is an ancient goddess mostly associated with love, music, dance, intoxication and drunkenness. Like Set, she is an ancient stellar deity ie she is a star goddess just as he is a star god. Hathor is said to possess a "Book of Fate" something clearly related to astrological lore. In it she inscribes a person's name and indeed fate at birth. When one's time is up she dispatches one of her seven adversaries or reapers, known as the Hatayou, to gather the soul, a function that we cannot help but see as demonic. In Egyptian religious texts these are also referred to as "flower cutters" by reason of the flint knives. Flint was a substance often associated with the god Set.

Hathor's connection with these demons seems to link her with a mythos of much later times the North African Zar cult? This healing cult is still practiced in many parts of Egypt. Its foundation myth records an origin in ancient Egypt. The victim is struck down by a demonic messenger, almost invariable a troublesome ancestor who cannot be driven out by aggressive exorcism, but needs a more subtle approach. Basically the demon is brought on side during a special party, which features the characteristic Zar music and dance, but also feasting on freshly slaughtered meat.

In ancient times one of the most important tasks of the magician was to overcome the demons of fate, literally to remove names from Hathor's book. Magick is here the opposer of fate. All of which suggests something called the "demonic initiation" that is to say an initiation that involved perfection by knowing what the demons and their mistress know about you, and making them forget (exorcism). Knowing thyself may mean knowing what is written in your stars. With this knowledge or *gnosis* the magician is prepared to make his or her own fate.

Why is Seth Demonic initiator?

Charlotte, knowing as she does that Set is my personal obsession wonders if he is really relevant here. I have to say like so much it's all serendipity, luck and arbitrary choice. But there again is that really any worse a guide than other approaches? After all the seemingly random choice and serendipity did lead us into some interesting, ambiguous territory.

Egyptian "theology" teaches that pretty much all deities are highly ambiguous even androgynous entities with what we would recognise as strong "demonic" tendencies. In the Egyptian magical religion the daemons are related to particular stars; and Set is the stellar deity who as the constellation The Plough, leads them all in their diurnal cycle.

So who is Set? He was and for many still is one of humanity's oldest gods, a cosmic entity whose origins are lost in the Neolithic – his cult already ancient at the time of the unification of Egypt (3100BC). To me he is a pre or (pan) cultural entity and belongs to the universal strata of Mind.

In addition to his old time stellar role he is one of the original lunar gods. Set's lunar credentials are further underlined by myths in which he gives birth to Thoth, also a moon god. The moon has strong connections with tides, terrestrial and cosmic. It gives its name to the period of 30 days we call a month.

It is widely recognised that Set's androgynous personality makes him especially relevant and important for our new Aquarian age or

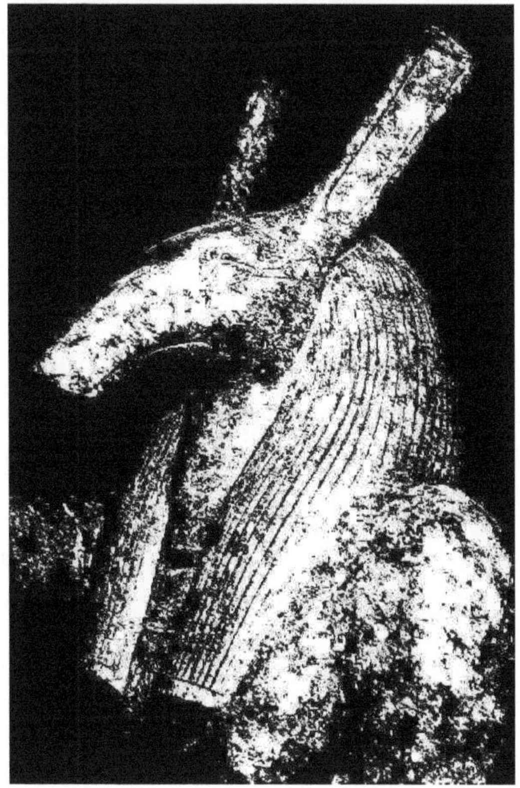

Thelemic Aeon. He has male and female characteristics, which has been interpreted in the modern world as encompassing heterodox sexualities. Egyptian mythology presents this in terms of a "homosexual" episode in which he attempts to seduce his brother. In this lies the core of a magical secret that has tantalised magicians and mythographers ever since it was first recorded. Set swallows his brother's seed and performs the quintessential female act – he gives birth. It is perhaps less well known that other gods also possess this power. The equally androgynous Atum-Ra, "father" of the gods, fulfils his creator function by first masturbating then swallowing his own seed.

The functions of a god like Set are hidden and often not something that jumps out. The revelation of his mysteries often comes by the reversal of commonplace views – it involved uncommon sense. Perhaps this is why his cult is so often involved with demons and what has been termed the crooked wand or way.

Furthermore demonic initiation may be indirect, perhaps brought about by random coincidence and the seemingly odd. That's why I thought demonic initiation must be related to "exorcism". The meaning of the term exorcism has changed slightly in modern use – its gnostic component downplayed. Ancient exorcism can be likened more to a process of de-conditioning of a kind familiar in the later, and I'd say related, cult of Tantra.

The modern rediscovery of a Thelemic rite known as *Liber Samech* seems to me to be equally infused with coincidence. It began life as an ancient rite of exorcism but is now inextricably linked with the quest for one's Holy Guardian Angel! Not surprisingly then that I and several other progressive magicians have detected the presence of the god Set in its mythology.

In conclusion

I have tried to dispense with much cultural detail and seek the universal pattern – something that speaks directly to the living phenomenon that is the magician. In doing so I have ventured into the realm of the god Set and explored the theme of ambiguity. From ambiguity it is a short step to a demonology of transactions between, gods and daemons often involving the shedding of blood. I have also drawn attention to an alternative to the shedding of human and perhaps even animal blood, one that is sanctioned by antiquity. So what better point to end than with a few lines of the already mentioned rite of exorcism, that for some appears negative and for others holds the key to liberation:

"Subject to me all daimons / so that every daimon,
whether of the heavens
of the air
of the earth
the underworld
or terrestrial
or aquatic,
might be obedient to me
and every enchantment and scourge which is from God."

(PGM V 96-172)

Sources

Professor John Baines "Ankh Sign, belt and penis sheath" *ZAS* bd 3 1975 (in Pamphlet box 2)

Gregory Reeder (2005) "The Eunuch and the Wab Priest: another look at the mysterious Manchester Mummies" *KMT* pp54-65

See also *Hathor Rising* (Hathor's Secrets) Alison Roberts

David, R (2007) *The Two brothers, Death and the Afterlife in Middle Kingdom Egypt.*

Hornung, Erik (1999) *Ancient Egyptian Books of the Afterlife*, translated by David Lorton, Cornell

Margaret Murray (1910) *The Tomb of the Two Brothers*, anatomical report by Dr John Cameron.

Morgan, M (2011) Supernatural Assault in Ancient Egypt, Mandrake.

Westendorf, Wolfhart (1966) *Beiträge aus und zu der medizinischen Texten,* (Contributions from and to the medical texts) 151-4 , ZAS 92

Petrie, F (1892), *Medum,* Comment of Sayce on page 33.

Carolyn Graves-Brown (ed.), *Sex and Gender in Ancient Egypt*: 'Don your wig for a joyful hour'. Swansea: Classical Press of Wales, 2008. see: Greg Reeder, "Queer Egyptologies of Niankhkhnum and Khnumhotep" (pp. 143-155):

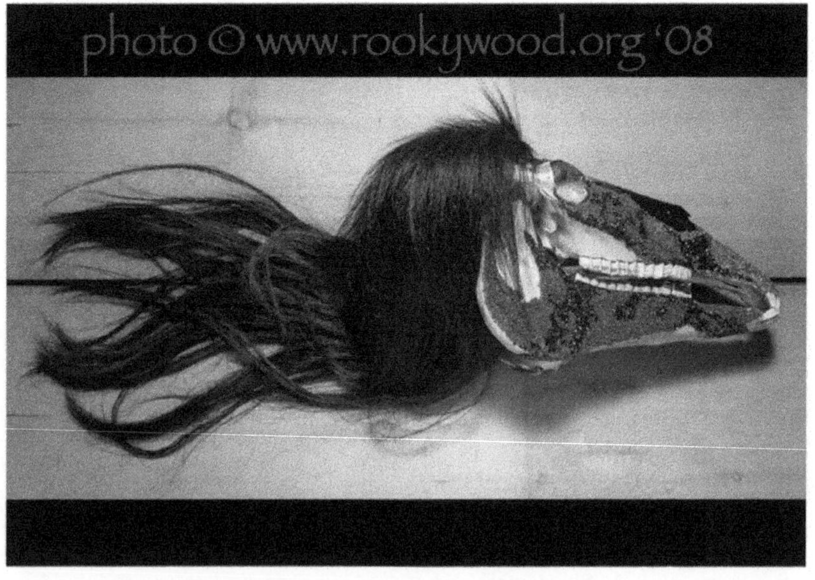

'N'Mare. Mixed media with horses skull made by Charlotte Rodgers

Table 1: Correspondences: Essential Nature of Sacramental Offerings

	Psychology	*Meditation*	*Feeding Spirits/ God Forms*	*Rites*	*Art*	*Initiatory Ability*
Menstrual Blood (applies to both genders)	Curiosity about the menstrual cycle is a healthy facet of awareness about self and ones place within nature.	Working with menstruation highlighted my connectivity with nature and the moon's cycle. It assisted my learning how different sorts of consciousness are more accessible at various moon phases. It was also interesting working with the concept of	Works well with no problems. Very effective when working with chthonic forms.	Due to blood borne illness care is needed, but otherwise works well in group rituals and for bonding of any sort. Good with spell craft esp. binding and curses.	Effective with no real issues. Great for mixing with clay especially.	Yes

		gender in God and Spirit forms at different times of the menstrual cycle and corresponding moon phases. I also successfully used menstrual blood with my mirror meditation and journeying work .				
Live Sacrifice	n/a	n/a	n/a	n/a	n/a	n/a

Tattooing/ Scarification	Ostensibly decorative, in actuality it acts as a mark of belonging or indication of a rite as passage or healing. Definitely mood altering and can be addictive.	Creates a dislocation from the body.	This comes as a huge commitment as it's a lifelong relationship! Works superbly if this is the case.	Ritualised these acts are incredibly powerful especially as initiatory rites.	Very effective.	Yes
Human Blood	Creates an altered state in its release and an escape from the mundane. This can be an addictive process.	Very effective but I had to maintain vigilance to differentiate between being in a meditation or trance state. Post any blood loss there is also a huge	Very problematic as Gods and Spirits greatest desire is to be given life. Feeding of human blood can create obsession and vociferous demands	The obvious care is needed re blood borne illness, but it can prove a very powerful tool to use in rituals	This can be very problematic in its ability to give life to the inanimate.	Yes

		energetic weakness on every level, which one must be aware of and deal with.	from that which is being fed. A strong sense of self in such workings is necessary as confusion between one's own wishes and that of spirits can occur. Areas where blood is spilled (hospitals and battlefield) can often have a chaotic energy caused by spirits hanging around looking to feed.	working with creating a bond with other ritualists.		

Bone	Represents death and the transience of mortality.	Useful as an aid to confront fears of death, and as a gateway between the worlds. Wonderful to work with the essence of a species and to in case of violent death, meditate on healing restless and uneasy spirits.	I've never found it good as a food per se, although as a material to make an offering, excellent.	Some of my most powerful rituals have used bones as an aid to call forth spirits or as a link between the worlds. It is a superb medium to make spirit houses from	As the bone holds the memory of the species it is useful to work with creatively as I can channel the energy of the animal into the art.	Yes

Table 2: Correspondences: Essential Nature of Species

	Qualities	*Purpose*		*Practise*
Pig	Earthy focus.	Material aspects of a creative project.		*Prosperity Pig,* a variation of a spirit house which I created to confront and challenge outdated concepts of material gain being representative of greed.
Horse	Harnessing and directing of base instinct, working with liminal energy.	Transformation on an emotional level. Working with the shadow self. Journeying work.		*N'Mare, The Descent* was designed to work with the trauma of chemotherapy in the manner of a traditional shamanic journey.
Fox	Youthful playful and focused; the trickster magickian.	Healing of the child self.		Teeth of a young fox were given to a friend who had lost vigour and joy due to long term illness.
Birds	Smaller birds are great for representing the frail beauty of the early stage of a creative enterprise. Larger birds represent fulfilment direct intentions with no emotional involvement	Success with creative projects (smaller birds). Larger birds for focus and wisdom and ability to rise above mundane trivia to success.		A mummified goldfinch was placed at the centre of my Kali altar representative of the fragile beauty of love and early stages of a creativy that must be protected and nurtured in order to develop. The finch was surrounded by a pair of crows wings representing a focused and wilder side of the species that will destroy anything that threatens love. .

Domesticated Animals	I personally do not like working with animals that have been domesticated as I find their specific species are often muddled with the energy of their human owners.	Although I do not usually work with these creatures I recently used the bones of a domesticated animal to add an element of fidelity to an adoration icon which I was making for a feminine god form.		I combined the disparate elements of a domestic cat with a crow in a sculpture to create ability to rise above feelings of submission to contemporary society.
Human	Communication with the dead.	A gateway to aspects of dead humanity, either on an individual level or as a learning tool.		I used remnants of human bone as a gateway to communicate with the dead.

Bibliography

Crowley, Aleister, 1976, *The Book of the Law* (Samuel Weiser).

Dalrymple, William, 2009, *Nine Lives* (Bloomsbury).

Eliade, Mircea, 1965, *Mephistopheles and the Androgyne* (New York, Sheed and Ward).

Evola, Julius, 1983, *The Metaphysics of Sex* (East-West Publications).

Favazza, Armado R, 1996, *Bodies under Siege: Self Mutilation and Body Modification in Culture and Psychiatry*, Baltimore and London (The John Hopkins University Press).

Fonseca, Isabel, 1995, *Bury Me Standing: The Gypsies and their Journey* (Random House, U.K).

Girard, Rene, 2007, *Violence and the Sacred* (London, New York, Continuum).

Grant, Kenneth, 1997, *Nightside of Eden* (Muller).

Grey, Peter, 2008, The *Red Goddess* (Scarlet Imprint).

Huxley, Francis, 1956, *Affable Savages* (London. Rupert Hart-Davies).

Kaldera, Raven, 2006, *Pagan BDSM and the Ordeal Path* (Hubbardston, MA.Asphodel).

Katzeff, Paul, 1988, *Moon Madness* (Citadel Press).

Diego de Landa, Friar, 1978, *Yucatan Before and After the Conquest* (New York, Dover).

Leyser, Henrietta, 1995, *Medieval Women: A Social History of Women in England 450-1500* (Phoenix Press, London).

Lindsay, Arturo (editor) 1996, *Santeria Aesthetics in Contemporary Latin American Art*, (Washington and London. Smithsonian).

Martinie, Louis and Sallie Ann Glassman, 1992, *New Orleans Voodoo Tarot* (Destiny Books).

Martine, Louis, *Talking to God with Food: the Question of Animal Sacrifice* (http://www.horusmaat.com/silverstar/SILVERSTAR1-PG31.html)

Mitamura, Taisuke, 1963, *Chinese Eunuchs the Structure of Intimate Politics*, (Tuttle).

Linden, Mishlen, 1993, *Typhonian Teratromas*, (Black Moon Publishing).

Neihardt, John G (as told to), 1979, *Black Elk Speaks*, Lincoln and London (University of Nebraska Press).

Phillips, Adam, 1996, *On Flirtation*, (Harvard University Press).

Phillips, Anita, 1998, *A Defence of Masochism*, (Kent. Faber and Faber).

Vale, V and Juno, A, 1989.*Modern Primitives*, (RE/Search).

Van Baaren, Th.P. Jan, 1964, *Theoretical Speculations on Sacrifice* (Numen, Vol 11, Fasc.1, pp1-12).

The Boston Women's Health Collective, 1998, *Our Bodies, Ourselves* (Touchstone Books).

Index

Mandrake - New Occultural Titles

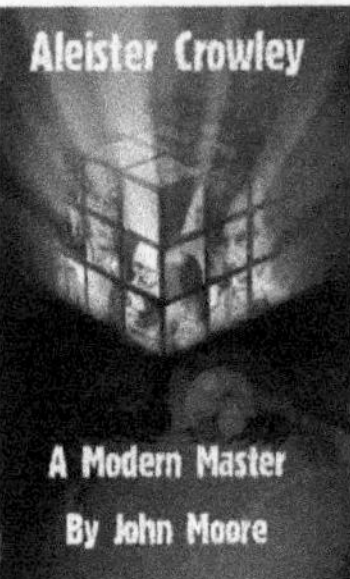

Aleister Crowley : A Modern Master - Placing the Beast in his cultural background By John Moore

ISBN 978-1-906958-02-2, £10.99, 216pp

Contents: Introduction / His Life / Crowleyan Romanticism / Crowley ar Protestantism / Repression / Directions / & Liberty / Raw will / Valu of Catholicism / Self negating decadence / French perspectives / Decadence Persecution / Luther / Calvin / Myth / Modern applications / England Russians / Morals / Wesley / Aleister Crowley and Philosophy / Kabbalah Magick / Philosophy proper / Crowley and Imperialism / Crowley's Sexu Stalinism / The Abbey / For all? / Cocaine / Liberation / Womanhoc / Conclusion / Aleister Crowley As Guru / Bibliography

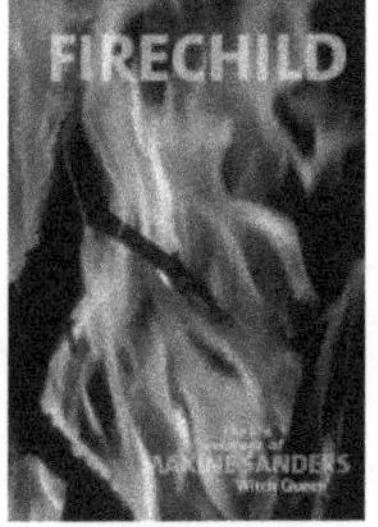

Fire Child - The Life and Magic of Maxine Sanders 'Witch Queen' By Maxine Sanders

ISBN 978-1869928-780, Paperback, £12.99/$26 312pp

In this long awaited autobiography, Maxine reflects on her life and magical care From her unusual and disturbing childhood, to her partnership with Alex Sande her joys and sorrows, her vocation and work as a Priestess of the Goddess, teach and spiritual catalyst. This is a memoir of an extraordinary life, by a rare, courageo and inspiring woman. *Fire Child* is pure magic. Don't miss it!

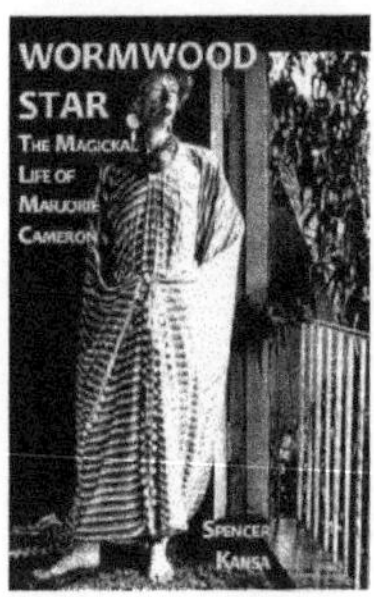

Wormwood Star - The Magickal Life Of Marjorie Cameron By Spencer Kansa, ISBN 978-1-906958-08-4, £12.99, 280pp, illustrated

In the first ever biography written about her, *Wormwood Star* traces the extraordina life of the enigmatic artist Marjorie Cameron (1922-1995), one of the mo fascinating figures to emerge from the American Underground art world and fil scene.

'Wormwood Star' is a book that I have been waiting for, for a long, long time...a definitive guide to this fascinating woman.. .social commentary as much as a riveting biography..." Charlotte Rodgers

Mandrake of Oxford
PO Box 250, Oxford, OX1 1AP (UK)
Phone: 01865 243671 for free catalogue & credit card sales

Prices include economy postage
online at - www.mandrake.uk.net
Email: mandrake@mandrake.uk.net

Lightning Source UK Ltd.
Milton Keynes UK
UKHW010727080320
359958UK00001B/26

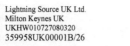

9 781906 958305